ROSINA MARIA ARQUATI
The Life Journey of an Animal Communicator

"For Our Brothers and Sisters in the Animal Kingdom"
"May We Be Truer Friends to Animals"

Rosina Maria Arquati

BALBOA.
PRESS
A DIVISION OF HAY HOUSE

Copyright © 2013 Rosina Maria Arquati.

All rights reserved. No part of this book may be used or reproduced by any means, graphic, electronic, or mechanical, including photocopying, recording, taping or by any information storage retrieval system without the written permission of the publisher except in the case of brief quotations embodied in critical articles and reviews.

Balboa Press books may be ordered through booksellers or by contacting:

Balboa Press
A Division of Hay House
1663 Liberty Drive
Bloomington, IN 47403, USA
www.balboapress.com.au
1-(877) 407-4847

ISBN: 978-1-4525-8320-4 (sc)
ISBN: 978-1-4525-8319-8 (hc)
ISBN: 978-1-4525-8328-0 (e)

Library of Congress Control Number: 2013917523

Because of the dynamic nature of the Internet, any web addresses or links contained in this book may have changed since publication and may no longer be valid. The views expressed in this work are solely those of the author and do not necessarily reflect the views of the publisher, and the publisher hereby disclaims any responsibility for them.

The author of this book does not dispense medical or veterinary advice; and does not prescribe the use of any technique as a form of treatment for physical, emotional, or medical problems without the advice of a physician or veterinarian as relevant. You should always obtain professional veterinary examination and advice for your animals, and professional medical examination and advice for yourself.

The intent of the author is only to offer information of a general nature to help in your quest for emotional and spiritual well-being. In the event you use any of the information in this book, the author and the publisher assume no responsibility for your actions.

Any people depicted in stock imagery provided by Thinkstock are models, and such images are being used for illustrative purposes only. Certain stock imagery © Thinkstock.

Printed in the United States of America

Balboa Press rev. date: 10/24/2013

CONTENTS

Preface. v

Important Note vii

About Rosina ix

Part I: My Life Story

Chapter 1:   The Journey Begins 1

Chapter 2:   A Little Girl With A Gift. 7

Chapter 3:   Happy Times 13

Chapter 4:   Things Change. 16

Chapter 5:   Teen Times. 19

Chapter 6:   Hong Kong, Our New Home. 26

Chapter 7:   The Animals Keep Coming 32

Chapter 8:   Many Species Need Care 38

Chapter 9:   Moving again 48

Chapter 10: Baby Primates 50

Chapter 11: From the twentieth century into the twenty-first 56

Chapter 12: The Aristocratic Pomeranians Come Into My Life. 59

Chapter 13: Animal Communication Grows 73

Chapter 14: Life is a Circle. 77

Chapter 15: Continuing the Journey 80

Part II: Foundations of Animal Communication

Chapter 16: Introducing Animal Communication 83

Chapter 17: Basic Concepts. 89

Chapter 18: Experience animals and nature. 91

Chapter 19: Exercises to Get You Started 94

Chapter 20: Visualization Exercise............................ 102
Chapter 21: Animals that have passed away.................... 107
Chapter 22: Do animals lie?................................. 112
Chapter 23: Sharing some Animal Communication
             Experiences With You............................ 115
Chapter 24: Let's Chat 126
Chapter 25: Ethics... 132
Chapter 26: Q&A: Questions & Answers 136
Chapter 27: Dimensions of Communication 142
Chapter 28: Energy Healing 147
Chapter 29: Animal Welfare 155
Chapter 30: Keep On, Don't Give Up.......................... 165

Part III: Appendix

Animal Communication Practice Log Sheets..................... 171
Acknowledgements... 173

PREFACE

In this age and time, with so much modern technology, more people are seeing the need to recognize their connection with all living beings. With the teachings of animal communication, communications between humans and animals have taken on a deeper meaning.

Animals provide us with one of the best educations we can ever have in life. Animal Communication uses telepathy to communicate with animals, creating a deeper bond and understanding between humans and animals, providing us with the balance many of us require in our lives.

Animals communicate with each other via telepathy, as well as body language and vocalization, using the transmission of feelings, intentions, thoughts, mental images, emotions and sensations. All humans were born telepathic but, with the changes in society, complex verbal and written language has become the main human tool for communication. However, we can be taught animal communication and how to tune in and perceive what the animals are telling us.

If you have ever thought that you heard your pet "say" something to you, you could be right! Animals are able to communicate with humans who are open to the connection. They understand your intentions, emotions, images, thoughts, tones behind your words—even if they can't fully understand all the words used.

In this book, I sometimes describe communications written in a form like human dialogue, for example, "Hallo," said the cat. This is to make it easier for readers to understand the communications. In reality the communications took place in the ways outlined in Part II of this book. But an experienced animal communicator receives messages and understands them much as he/she would understand conversation received from another human.

You can learn animal communication; it is simple but does require persistence and practice. You need to put aside your mind barriers and discard any attitude of thinking that animals are less intelligent than us. Move forward with your love for animals and a willingness to learn to connect with animals.

In Part I of this book, I will tell you about my life journey to become an animal communicator, and some of my experiences with animals and animal communication from an early age up to the present.

In Part II, I will cover some of the foundations and basics for beginning animal communication, as well as matters of animal welfare.

Namaste
Rosina

IMPORTANT

Animal Communication is complementary to other modalities, and helps you to better understand animals. It is *never* a substitute for professional veterinary advice and treatment. You should continue to consult your veterinarian.

Animal Communication needs ongoing practice and progression. You will not master it overnight, or just by reading this book. But you can make a start if you have an interest. With time and practice and understanding, your abilities can gradually develope, progress and improve. Do not jump to conclusions about animals; keep an open mind. Never put yourself or others in a position of real or potential danger.

WILD ANIMALS

Some of the stories and cases in this book relate to wild animals and/ or animals in international endangered species recovery programmes. Together with Rosina's special compassion and communication, all of these animals were under on-going veterinary care and treatment by veterinarians experienced with such animals. All the wild animals were rescued animals under veterinary treatment and rehabilitation care.

The welfare of each and every animal was and is paramount at all times.

Wild animals are not suitable as pets. Exploitation of wild animals for the pet trade is NOT condoned: it is harmful to the animals, and is generally contrary to basic animal welfare concepts and conservation.

ABOUT ROSINA

Rosina has made her home in Hong Kong for over 35 years. She lives there with her veterinarian husband and rescued animals. Rosina is experienced in Animal Communication, and in teaching this; as well as energy healing for animals.

She was the first teacher to teach Animal Communication in Hong Kong S.A.R China. She also teaches in Singapore, Malaysia, Taiwan and elsewhere in Asia, as well as in Hong Kong. Rosina is a Member of the New Zealand Charter of Practitioners (since 1996).

She is the Founder and Director of Animal Talk Ltd, as well as being the Founder of the AACCA [Alliance of Animal Communicators Caring about Animals].

A natural born animal communicator, her skills have been developed over many years, from childhood on. She enhances her natural animal communication skills with natural healing modalities.

Clients come to Rosina with problems about their pets, and while communicating with the animals(s) Rosina will help guide the client to better understand the animal(s) and move towards solving the problems. This special gift of Animal Communication is enhanced by energy healing for animals and humans.

Rosina teaches Animal Communication, in workshops and classes, in Hong Kong and in other countries.

She also helps clients by bereavement counseling when they have lost their pets through illness, accident or old age, which helps them overcome the grief that they feel when they lose their pets. Rosina is the Founder of AACCA (Alliance of Animal Communicators Caring about Animals), in which her students and former students fundraise for animal charities at charity events, and at the same time introduce people to Animal Communication concepts with Animal Welfare. In addition, Animal Talk Ltd, of which Rosina is Director and Founder, makes monthly donations to charities supported by Rosina.

She is a Member of the New Zealand Charter of Practitioners Inc, and is the Founder and Director of Animal Talk Ltd. She is a Reiki Master, and holds a Certificate of Teaching Standards New Zealand Reiki, Certificate of Membership New Zealand Reiki and Certificate of Accreditation New Zealand Reiki (since 1996); and is a Member of IARP® (the International Association of Reiki Professionals®). She is an Usui Reiki Master/Teacher, Karuna Master/Teacher, Seichim Master/Teacher, Magnified Healing™ Practitioner/Teacher, Crystal Healing Practitioner/Teacher, Angel Intuitive Practitioner/Teacher, and Advanced Energy Healing. She is also certificated in Colour Therapy for Animals, and in TTouch.

Her life journey has been enhanced by travel through Asia and elsewhere, opening people's hearts to the Animal Kingdom, acknowledging that animals are our best friends. A natural animal communicator, she helps people to understand that animals have feelings and emotions. This understanding helps to reduce abandonment of animals, and enhances animal welfare. Rosina is spending her life in connecting people with animals, and working for the higher good of people and animals.

Rosina Maria Arquati
Animal Talk Ltd

Animal Communicator and Animal Healer
Animal Communication Workshops/Classes
Bereavement Counselor

Phone (mobile)	(+852) 6089 4727 (English, Cantonese, Mandarin/ Putonghua)
Landline	(+852) 2549 3332 (English)
Email	animaltalk8@gmail.com
Website	http://rosina.wordpress.com
China web	http://blog.sina.com.cn/animaltalk

Come and Join Rosina Arquati Facebook (Official):
http://www.facebook.com/rosina.arquati
http://www.facebook.com/#!/pages/Animal-Talk-Asia/15536
1161293637

Main email address   (international)
animaltalk8@gmail.com

Local email addresses
Hong Kong: animaltalk8@gmail.com
Taiwan: animaltalktw@gmail.com
Malaysia: animaltalkmalay@gmail.com
Singapore: animaltalksg@gmail.com
China: animaltalkchina@gmail.com

PART I
My Life Story

CHAPTER 1

The Journey Begins

Where does one start? For me, it is with my grandparents. My grandfather, Sevorino Marino, was an interesting character. Born in Italy in the 1880s, he spent his childhood growing up in a poor Italian family in the province of Avellino.

At the age of fourteen, Sevorino left Italy with his twelve year old brother, travelling by sea to America hoping for a better life. These two boys with big dreams, seeking a new life where dreams could really come true, arrived in America within sight of the Statue of Liberty. My grandfather's brother decided to settle in Philadelphia growing mushrooms, while my grandfather had dreams of becoming a "Mountie" in the Royal Canadian Mounted Police.

So my grandfather Sevorino made his way to Canada. But his dream was short lived. He could not read or write and could not be a Mountie. He started to walk around the streets, trying to learn the numbers from the doors and using the street names in his attempts to learn to read; but he was unable to learn in this way. What he did not know was that he was dyslexic, something that would run in the family for generations. So, still a young man, he left Canada and travelled to France, where he met a young French girl who gave him a son. My grandfather wanted to go to England, but the French girl did not want to leave France, so he left his first love and

Rosina Maria Arquati: The Life Journey of an Animal Communicator

moved to England where he settled down in the area known as Little Italy, which was Clerkenwell in London. It was the early twentieth century now.

Tall, slim and handsome as a young man, Grandfather Sevorino was very attractive to the ladies of "Little Italy". He was also regarded as being gifted in the art of healing and able to understand people's worries.

Work opportunities in London were limited as he had difficulty with reading and writing. Asphalting came up as a work opportunity, and so he took this as his job. However, he discovered that people were coming to him for advice and healing. He continued his life as a simple ashphalter, but people continued to come to him for healing and advice.

London is where my grandmother, Maria, enters the story. Also born in the 1880s in Italy, she was a lady whose mother had died when she was young in Italy, and her father, still in Italy, remarried. His new wife did not want Maria, so she was very cruel to her.

Later on, my grandmother Maria and her half-brother were brought to England where my grandmother was made to work and live at an Italian grocery shop. My grandfather Sevorino would go into the grocery shop to buy cigarettes. Soon he fell in love with this kind gentle young lady, Maria. In due course, he wanted to marry her, but the owners of the shop would not let her go. When the shop owners finally did agree to let her go, they refused to pay her. My grandfather then stepped in, and my grandmother got paid.

This loving couple, my grandfather and grandmother, married. They produced ten children, five survived and five died. In 1918 my grandmother gave birth to their fifth child, a girl, my future mother Delena. In all, they produced ten children. Five of their children survived and five died. The family lived together in Clerkenwell, London, raising the five surviving children.

It was the custom of my grandfather to make wine from grapes every year. The job of pressing the grapes in the large barrels fell to the children, who would sing and dance as they trod the grapes. Grandmother always smiled as she watched her children, but deep inside she was sad about the five other children whom she lost at childbirth.

Grandfather had the gift of foreseeing what was going to happen, and he possessed the gift of healing. People would come to him for help and for healing. He also loved to cook, and to drink his home made wine. Often, he would cook dinner for the local priest, and, after the priest left, he would hold healing groups and medium circles.

Grandfather Sevorino

Grandmother, on the other hand, was a quiet lady. Her family and home were the most important things to her. She was also gifted with a connection to animals, and when my mother brought home a black dog, my grandmother connected with this doggy.

"Rover", the dog, became the most important thing in my grandmother's life until she died. Even now, she and Rover are inseparable in the spirit world where they are together.

Grandmother Maria with cat and mother Delena with Rover the dog

After the Second World War, the family moved to Islington, also in London. It was here that grandfather died.

Before he died, Grandfather Sevorino felt the need to call in the priest on three separate occasions to administer the last rites. After the priest had left following the second occasion of the rites, my grandfather told his eldest son Camilo that there were four angels around the bed where grandfather lay, one at each corner of his bed. One of the angels, grandfather told my uncle Camilo, was the Angel Michael. Michael told my grandfather that the angels would not let him into the Kingdom of Heaven yet. Camilo then told my grandfather that he must confess everything.

When the priest came for the third time, grandfather Sevorino confessed everything. He then told Camilo that the angels had opened the Gates of Heaven. Then grandfather slowly passed over.

I never knew my grandfather: he died before I was born.

After the loss of her husband, my grandmother's life seemed empty: an empty feeling also shared by her daughter Delena, my mother. My mother went on to have an affair with a handsome young Italian man living in London. His name was Ettore, though he was widely known as "Johnny", and, in a day of passion, I was conceived. For a good Catholic girl like my mother, this was a sin. All hell let loose when she finally told the family that she was pregnant.

My father, Johnny, was already married to someone else and could not marry my mother. Instead, he paid for her to go into a nunnery for unmarried mothers. This, my mother later told me, was the best time in her life. She learned from the nuns there how to "tell fortunes" using playing cards, and during her pregnancy she developed a craving for peaches which were difficult to find in 1950s London.

When it came to the time for her to give birth, I did not want to come out. Mum was in labour for a very long time. Eventually, at twelve midnight on a cold night in midwinter, she signed permission for forceps to be used to bring me into this world. Then, at ten minutes past midnight, I was born, a nine pound baby girl.

My mother was happy taking care of her new baby, but the family decreed that she could not keep the baby. So I was taken away from her and sent to a foster home in Southall, London. This distressed my mother, who did not want to lose me, and so she left the family and went to get me back. This caused the family to change their minds, and they decided that she could bring me home. My grandmother felt too old to look after me without help. My mother had to go out to work, and so a Jewish lady who lived next door also helped to look after me.

With me back in the family, my grandmother began to love me. Her favourite place for me to be with her was in the kitchen, where she would cook wonderful Italian food.

But life does not always run smoothly. One day, just ten months after my birth, my grandmother went out to buy food at the local Italian shop. As she set out on her way, she waved to me as she passed the house next door where I was playing, and called out "Arrivederci Rosina" ("See you later, Rosina," in the Italian language). But she never came home. A van hit her as she crossed the road, and grandmother died on that cold rainy autumn day.

She died intestate, and my mother's life changed dramatically from the moment my grandmother was no longer there to protect us. We now became lodgers in the family home as my aunt and uncle took control of it.

Mother was still finding it hard being a woman on her own with a small child, and, when an old boyfriend came back into her life, she agreed to marry him. Things were good before they married, but once they were married he did not want me in mother's apartment in the family house. He also started to drink excessively. Once again, my mother had to be strong, and she made him leave.

However, she continued to use her married name from this man, who was named Mr Burrows, and I grew up with the surname Burrows, no longer using my father's name of Arquati.

As my mother had to go out to work, she found a nursery for me when she was working. I was always the last child to leave the nursery as mum had to work late.

CHAPTER 2

A Little Girl With A Gift

My life passion in communicating with animals started when I was very young. Gifts are given in many different ways, and mine was connecting with the animal kingdom.

As a child I tried to tell people that I could talk to animals, but they just told me not to be silly. So I kept quiet. In chakra theory, my throat chakra became blocked, predisposing me to tonsillitis, so that I spent much time in hospital then. It was during a spell in hospital that I remember my first true animal communication.

I was about five years old. It was winter, and because of my tonsillitis I was in hospital again. I spent many winters in hospital as a child, and many Christmases there.

The children's ward was full, so I was put into an adult ward for women. Opposite to me was a lady with a lovely smile. The nurse would not allow me to get out of bed until the fever went down. It would take some time for my fever to go down. The lovely lady would always smile at me. One night I was crying, and she called out to me and told me that I was safe. The next day, she asked the nurse if they would bring her over to me, and they did. She was very weak, and I knew that she was very ill, but as a child I did not know how ill. We talked all afternoon and she told me about her dog. We did not have modern technology then, and taking photographs was not as common then as it is now, so she did not have photographs with her.

As she talked about her dog, I heard the dog talk to me. "Tell mummy I love her very much and want to come and see her, before she goes."

I did not understand what the dog meant, but, as children do, I just told her, "Your dog loves you very much and wants to see you before you go".

The lady's eyes filled with tears and she said that she was not sure whether that would be possible.

I asked her why he could not come during visiting hours.

She said: "But Rosina, he's a dog".

"He's your son," I said, "Tell the nurses he's coming".

She just smiled, but her eyes were still filled with tears. When the nurse came to take her back to her bed the tears were still in her eyes.

After the nurse had put her back to bed, we were getting ready for visiting hour. I called out to her, "Your husband can bring your dog, because the dog told me that he cannot get here on his own". She must have thought "What a strange little girl".

The nurse told me that the lady was very sick and could not come to visit me anymore. I was very sad and remember saying that her son wanted to come to see her. The nurse said the lady did not have any child. "Oh, her dog is her son," I said. "Is he coming?" The nurse smiled.

A few days later, I saw the lady's husband outside talking to the matron, and I could hear the dog saying "I am here". I wanted to get out of bed to go and see the dog, but the nurse told me "Rosina get back into bed!" The door of the ward opened, the lady's husband came in carrying a small long dog. I crawled to the foot of my bed. "Rosina get back in bed!" ordered the matron, who was now standing by my bed, "Get into bed now Rosina!" They drew the curtain around the lady's bed and the lady's husband and dog stayed with her for some time.

On the way out, the husband and dog looked sad.
I said to the dog, "You saw your mummy?"
"Yes" came back the dog, "but she is not coming home and this is the last time I will see her, as she is very sick."
"But you can come again; visiting time is every day," I told him.

Then they left, the nurse drew the curtain back from the lady's bed, and the ward went back to normal.

I crawled to the bottom of my bed, and called out to the lady, "Your dog says he loves you very very much, but he says you are very sick." She gave me a lovely smile, as if she knew.

A few days later when I woke up, the lady's bed was empty. There had been a lot of noise in the ward that night, and all the curtains had been drawn. Then, in the early hours of the morning, the nurses were very quiet. I looked around the ward. She had not been moved to another part of the ward. The nurse knew that I was looking for her. Suddenly, I felt the matron standing by me. She bent over and told me that the lady had died in the night. "Oh," I responded, "that means she has gone to heaven. She can meet my grandmother there. Her dog told me that it would be the last time he would see her, but she can always pop back from heaven to see him, just like my grandmother comes to see me". The matron looked surprised, and said "That's right, Rosina".

Some days later, the lady's husband came back to visit me. He had brought with him a stuffed toy as a present for me. It was a long brown dog with a big head and a short body. It looked like the lady's dog. He sat down beside my bed. He was very quiet and sad.

"Before she died, my wife asked me to get this for you," he said.

"It looks like your dog," I replied.

"Yes," he said, "my wife told me that you talk to our dog."

Then he said he had to leave.

I kept that toy dog until I was about 19 years old. Somehow the toy became lost when we moved house. But the sweet smile from the lady has always stayed in my heart.

It was at the age of five that I had my first wedding! One of the teachers at the nursery school got married. As she could not invite all the children to her wedding, she organized a faux wedding at the nursery. The teacher appointed two of the children to be the bride and groom, The wedding clothes were made by the children from crepe paper. I was the bride. The young man I "married" was named David, a premonition of things to come!

My Faux Wedding Age 5 at School

Rosina Maria Arquati: The Life Journey of an Animal Communicator

The next encounter I remember in talking to animals came to me when I was a little older, six or seven. My aunt owned and ran the Arsenal Café in Highbury, London, and when the Arsenal football team was playing at home, mum would help in the shop. I was too young to help in the café, as it became very crowded and I could get squashed, so I was sent to the back room. In those days, the television programmes did not start until 5pm, and we were not allowed to switch on the television unless there was an adult around. So I would stay in the room by myself. With the coal fire roaring, I stayed as close to it as possible. I have always hated cold weather.

Looking into the fire I would think of living on a warm tropical island. I remember speaking out "I want to live somewhere warm, I hate the winter."

A reply came to me: "I will come with you; where shall we go?"
I looked round. Nobody was there. Then, rubbing his body against my leg was my cousin's black cat.

I looked at him. "Is that you talking?"

"Yes," said the cat, "it is far too cold, where shall we go?"

"Well," I said, "maybe Italy, because that is where my family originally came from."

My cousin's black cat and I spent many winters together talking of travel to hot places.

Once when I went to visit my auntie and cousin, her black cat was missing. My cousin was upset. I suggested that we should try to find him. We went into the garden and called his name, but he did not come back. My cousin had to go to her piano practice lessons. I sat down in the garden quietly and asked the black cat to come home as everybody was worried about him. He would not be in trouble for running away, and we just wanted him home, as we loved him so much . . . . and who would I have to talk to on football days. Before long, I could hear his cat bell in the distance, and it was not long before he was next to me on the garden wall, purring and rubbing his body against my arm.

Happy Times

At that time, we lived in a big old house in Duncan Terrace in Islington, London. My mum and I had two big rooms upstairs, and my aunt and uncle lived downstairs with my two cousins. Life was good: three young girls growing up, playing on the terrace with our dolls and prams, my real father coming to visit me. My uncle made a big "dog house" in the garden where we children and the animals stayed together until late at night. Here it was normal for me to talk to the animals: I just thought it was what everyone did.

Those were happy days. I took my first Holy Communion while I was living there. I was given my first camera, a Brownie 127. Buzzy, the family dog, came into our lives. We enjoyed picnics in the garden, and sleepovers with the dog, cat and birds. This was the happiest part of my childhood. Yes, sometimes money was a little tight, and mum and I had to decide who would have the money: mum to get to work, or me for school.

One day, Buzzy the family dog was up in our part of the house. Mum was cooking Sunday lunch. I was not vegetarian then. Mum had made roast chicken. She left it on the table and went to get the vegetables. When she came back, Buzzy had stolen the chicken. We ran all round the house trying to get Buzzy to give us the chicken. I was out of breath running after Buzzy so I just sat down.

Rosina Maria Arquati: The Life Journey of an Animal Communicator

In my mind I asked Buzzy to give the chicken back to us.

He said: "Do you really want it back now, after I have been running around the house with it?"

"No, not really," I said, "I will tell mum you can have it."

"That sounds good," he said, "you don't really need it."

So Mum and I had a vegetarian lunch.

I was still in junior school. We had a fish tank in the classroom. I would talk to the fish in the morning when I got into school, and in the evening when we left. One of my classroom friends was called Teddy. He was a very academic boy, and we would get the bus home together every night. I am not sure how it happened, but the fish were dying. Teddy and I rushed to the fish tank to see what we could do. I told Teddy that the fish were saying that they could not breathe, and I asked him what we could do. We took the tank to the girls' changing room as we had big sinks in there, and we tried to save the fish. We tried very hard and it was dark when we had to give up. I remember crying when they died. Teddy and I buried the fish, and then went home by bus. I told Teddy that the fish told me that they wanted to live but they were in great pain. But it was time for them to go. Teddy told me, "We did our best," and I said "Yes."
When they left their bodies they said thank you to us for trying to help them.

Life was good then. We had holidays with another aunt and uncle and their two children at holiday camps. One year we had a caravan holiday. This is where I met sheep for the first time. The owners of the caravan site had a sheep farm. They kept two sheep as pets. I spent all my time with the sheep. We talked all day long, and even when I had to go home I did not want to leave my friends, the sheep. I went away crying. One sheep told me about her friends who went away and never came back. At that age I did not associate sheep with lamb chops. I told Miss Sheep that her friends must have gone to a new farm to live, but she said that they were dead. I really did not understand then, but I told her she was safe.

My mother had a job working in a café in Smithfield Meat Market in London. During school holidays, I would meet her there. She would ask me to collect the cups which customers had left in the market. I told my mum that I did not like going into the market as there were dead animals there. She said that the market was empty and all the meat had gone, but I responded that their spirits were still there.

One day, when I went into the market a side of beef was hanging up. As I ran in to collect the empty cups, I came face to face with this side of beef, which looked like almost half of a dead cow. I stopped. I froze. "Oh! You poor creature!" I said. Then tears came into my eyes. "Why did they do this to you!?" After this, I stopped eating beef.

My father was a butcher. He would make sure that we had a weekly supply of meat. My mum could not understand why I was not eating the meat. I tried to explain, but nobody would listen to me. At this stage I had stopped eating red meat but I was still eating chicken and fish.

Things Change

I continued to be in and out of hospital, and my school work was suffering. The main issue was that I could not spell. Back then, dyslexia was not understood. I was good at drawing and needle-work, so these were my main interests in class, except, of course, for my interest in boys.

So when it came to the important "eleven-plus" examination, I was in no way ready. The words just went blank. At the same time, my home life was changing dramatically, and that happy childhood stopped there and then. The family house in Islington was sold, and we moved in with my aunt in Tottenham, London. I told my mum: "Don't leave the family house!" I cried and cried. But someone was putting the frighteners on us. At night, there were strange noises in the garden and in the house, and my mother feared for our safety. So we moved to Tottenham. Life in Tottenham was very different from our life in Islington. Our two rooms in Tottenham were very small. I went to a school for girls there which was very different from my Catholic Convent school in Islington.

Our dog Buzzy was there with us, but life was not the same. Buzzy was great fun. He knew when the children were coming home from school and would wait at the local shop and ask the children for sweets, candies. He would wait for me to come to the corner shop, when he would tell me how many sweets he had been given and who he had met.

Then something happened! We children were told that Buzzy had been taken to a new home far away. No reason was given.

But Buzzy kept on telling me that he was not happy and he was going to come home. Sure enough, one day he turned up on the door step. I was so happy to see him. He was my best friend.

Finding his way home was the worst thing for Buzzy. He was far too loving and loyal to the family. One day, in school, I told my girl friend that something was wrong with Buzzy. He was being taken away again and said that he was going to die. After school, I asked my girl friend to rush out of school and run to the corner shop. Buzzy was not there. I went home. The house was in silence.

I asked my mum: "Where's Buzzy?"

She replied that he had been put to sleep. She did not know why, but said he would be safe now.

I asked: "Is he in heaven?"

But she responded, "Animals don't go to heaven."

So I told her: "Then I am not going to go to heaven either!"

I cried and cried. I just could not stop. I wondered why Buzzy had come home. He would still be alive if he had not returned. Then, a few weeks later, as I passed the corner shop I saw Buzzy sitting by the door of the shop. I heard him say, "I'm OK now, I have all the sweets I can eat. You need to look after yourself."

He was right. Things were getting bad. We were no longer welcome in the house in Tottenham. One night we found ourselves homeless, walking the streets in thick London fog, walking, just walking, with nowhere to go, until a man in a car picked us up and arranged for us to return to my aunt's house. We were only able to stay there for a week, until my mum found two attic rooms elsewhere where we could stay. Once again, Buzzy came to me in spirit. "You will be alright" he told me. "Don't be frightened." I told him about the night we walked the streets in the thick fog, and how frightened I was, but I remembered how brave he was when he found his way back.

So now we were living in two attic rooms, where my only "pets" were the mice who lived in the kitchen. We had a sofa bed which we would put down each night as we did not have a bedroom. Each night, when I got into bed, I would say in my mind "Goodnight" to Buzzy.

Me, at 13 years of age, in the garden of my best friend's family house in Tottenham, London, with Sammy the dog. Sammy belonged to my friend. At the time, I was quite "jealous" that my friend could have a dog when I couldn't!

Chapter 5

Teen Times

When we left Islington, my life became very different. We lived in two attic rooms. When it rained, the rain came in through the skylight, so we did not even have to look out of the window to see if it was raining. My friends were the mice, my little knights, always playing in the kitchen, where I spent time sitting.

I spent most of my time going to school because school was one of the best escapes I could have. I would arrive early and start work in the garden, collecting the flowers for the morning assembly and making the flower arrangements. I loved working in the garden amidst nature and the creatures that live in the natural world. And the cats would come to play in the garden, and I would play with them.

My dyslexia was a continuing difficulty. I simply could not spell. Fortunately, my history teacher understood the problem. She told me that there were children in higher classes who could not read or write, and that I was really bright, alert and intelligent. She helped me with my spelling, and I moved up to eighth-grade, where I had a wonderful English teacher. She was Scottish, and very very interesting. She was also very encouraging about my comprehension and my writing, but she was concerned about the length of the stories I wrote. For most children, she would ask them to write more, but, for me, she would ask me to write less because there were so many spelling mistakes that she had to correct. But she continued to encourage me to write because she told me that my stories were good and I needed to write. It was very hard for me to write, given my problems with spelling. She just laughed, and said: "Put pen to paper, and journey on that paper."

As a teenager in school, I spent a lot of time drawing and doing needlework as I really wanted to be a dress designer. That dream would not be realized. My mother and I did not have the money to send me to college for this, and we didn't know about getting a grant to pay for it. So when it was time to leave school, I had to seek employment. Secretarial work was out as I could not spell well. I had been on a few school visits to see various kinds of work places, where we school kids could see what things were like there.

On one school visit, we went to a posh department store in the West End of London, called Liberty's, which was very beautiful. The building had a Tudor style to it, and Liberty's was then a great fashion centre as one of London's most famous places for fabrics and designs. One of my friends had decided that she wanted to work at Liberty's, and I decided it would be a good idea for me too. So I applied, and was accepted.

On my first day at work I thought I would be working in the fashion section. There were two positions available when I joined Liberty's: one in the fashion/clothes department, and one in the bookshop. They decided that I should work in the bookshop because I had some library experience: I had previously been a display librarian, where I had arranged the displays of the books. Again, I was not happy, but the Universe had put me in the right place at the right time, and the bookshop turned out to be the right place for me. It gave me access to knowledge. Books contain knowledge: cookery books, gardening books, biographies, children's books, fiction, so many things to learn. I worked there alongside good friendly colleagues, and soon I became a part of the bookshop and enjoyed the knowledge that the books gave to me.

This is where I started my vegetarian journey. A book titled "Eating Your Way to Health" by Ruth Bircher-Benner came into the shop, and I started to read it. This opened my mind to understand that we do not need to eat meat, that is, we do not need to kill animals for us to eat healthily. Then I stopped eating meat. No more chicken, no more fish, no more dead animals on my plate. I started to learn about good nutrition and health, but my friends and family worried that I would die without meat!

Again, my life started to change. I decided that I needed to meet people with the same ideas as me, and so I joined the Young Vegetarian group in London, where there were lots of young people who were healthy and active and also cared about animals.

Sometimes this group would organize protests. At one protest, I helped put six girls, all wearing hotpants, into a cage in York to demonstrate against testing on animals and against vivisection laboratories. I didn't go in the cage: I worried that my legs were not good enough to display in hotpants, and that the other girls were prettier than me!

Joining the Young Vegetarians opened up my life. I met people, and I began to do a lot of vegetarian cooking. This was one of the exciting times in my life. I met people with the same belief systems as me and we were a young group who enjoyed going to discos, to theatres, to restaurants. It was a mixed group of boys and girls. We went on holiday, we laughed and we had fun like we should when we are 18 and 19 years old.

One day, one of the girls, a friend, introduced a young man to me. At the time I went under the surname Burrows, from my mother's married name, and my friend introduced him to me with the words: "Miss Burrows, meet Mr Burrows." I said, "Hello Mr Burrows." He responded, "And hello Miss Burrows." I looked up at him. He was tall, with a beard, and he had long curly hair. He did not seem very exciting to me. I was cooking in the kitchen at the time, so I continued, "Are you a food fan?" He replied," I like eating food, but I don't like food fanatics!" Then, after muttering "Nice to meet you," he acted on his words and wandered off into the other room to find food. He ate, he drank, and I thought "How boring." That was the end of our communications that evening.

Fate has a strange way of doing things. A year or two after that first meeting, one of my former boyfriends decided to hold an all night party in Maidenhead, England. I had no car and wondered how to get there, so he suggested that I should telephone one of the boys who did have a car. One of those telephone numbers turned out to be that of the aforementioned Mr Burrows, and I asked: "Hallo Mr B, I understand that you are going to the party in Maidenhead, and I wonder whether you could take my friend and me to the party in your car." He said that there was space available in his car, and yes he would be happy to drive us there. Arrangements were made to meet outside Liberty's, and off we went to the party. We enjoyed the evening together at the party, and the other girl went off with her boyfriend who turned up separately. After the party he drove me back home to London, and said he would phone me. His name was David.

It was mid-summer at the time, and he already had his summer holiday fixed, going to Sweden, as one of three male relay drivers of a 16-seater van full of teenage girls! So I thought I would never see him again.

However, it turned out that, when he returned to London, David did call me, and we started to date. This opened a big door for me because he brought animals back into my life in a very prominent way. He was a veterinarian, so his own life was filled with animals at work and at home. He was in private practice, and in addition to this he provided services to a home for abandoned dogs and for some animal welfare clinics. With him, I found myself again spending a lot of time with animals, both at his work and caring for his family animals with him. He did not find it strange that I talked with animals: he had already heard and read of this, he already had a close connection with animals in his life, and he was somebody who cared very deeply for animals.

Sooty the cat

Before my husband and I were married we used to spend time at his apartment at weekends. Of course, like all good girlfriends, I would cook lunch.

One day when I was in the kitchen preparing lunch, his black cat Sooty jumped up onto the kitchen work surface.

I said "Sooty, please get down, the only place I don't allow animals is where I am cooking."

Sooty replied: "No, I am not getting down, I am allowed to come up onto the cooking surface."

"No Sooty," I responded, "it is dangerous, if you come near me while I am preparing lunch I might accidentally cut your whiskers off."

"No you won't, don't be silly," she told me.

"Sooty, please get down from the cooking surface."

But she insisted on sitting there. I told her she needed to get down. At one stage I put her down and immediately she jumped up. "What do you think you are doing?" she said to me. "I am allowed to sit here."

"No, not when I am cooking," I said.

"David lets me come here when he is cooking," she said.

"It's different," I said.

"What are you going to do about it?" she responded.

"Well, if you don't get off I'll stop cooking till you get down."

"Okay then," she said.

It was a stalemate.

Sooty and I sat staring at each other, Sooty sitting firmly on the kitchen work surface and me on a stool.

Forty five minutes later when David returned home I burst out, "Your cat is very stubborn, she refuses to get down from the kitchen work surface."

David looked at me. Sooty stood up and walked along the work surface and brushed herself against his arm.

"I can't cook with a cat on the work surface, it's too dangerous, but she tells me that you let her up when you are doing the cooking, and she refuses to get down."

"Yes," he said, "I do let her up there."

"Fine," I said, "you'll be cooking lunch today."

The cat looked at me, went back to the corner, and sat down as David continued to prepare the Sunday lunch.

Engagement

Our relationship developed, and four years after our first date (that party in Maidenhead), we were engaged. About that time we also wanted to see more of the world. Several months later, David applied for, and was interviewed for, a job in Hong Kong. It was a tough interview, and he met me for lunch afterwards, convinced that he would not get the job. Nevertheless, a few months later a letter arrived in the post offering him the job, and he accepted. He was asked to turn up to work in Hong Kong as soon as possible: "We want you there yesterday," he was told. Six weeks was agreed as an alternative to attempting to arrive "yesterday"!

The Wedding

We were engaged but not yet married. The wedding was quickly arranged to be held in St Peter's Italian Church in London, as this was a tradition for my family. Only one priest at the Church could speak English, and so he was the priest who conducted our wedding as David wanted to be able to understand what was going on. The beautiful 19th century church organ played for the ceremony, a soloist sang *Ave Maria*, and one hundred wedding guests attended. As I walked down the aisle, I wondered whether I should go ahead and get married. But I had the right person, my soul partner for life. We both cared deeply about animals, and we would spend our lives together, develop together, and work together with animals as we both wanted the best for the animal kingdom. So, with a hundred witnesses in the church, we were wed.

Newly wed, outside the Church

Three days later, we were inside a jumbo jet at Heathrow airport, London, in a blizzard, the ground deep in snow. The runway was eventually cleared, and up we went into the sky albeit a few hours late.

It was not a direct flight as most aircraft could not fly non-stop from London to Hong Kong then. We were allowed to spend a few days as stopovers at each place where the aircraft landed en route, which were Italy and India. We visited the Vatican in Rome, the Taj Mahal in India, the Rajasthan desert, and the pink city of Jaipur. Then, on to Hong Kong which was to become our new home.

CHAPTER 6

Hong Kong, Our New Home

When we arrived, my husband was thrown into a busy work schedule with a wide variety of animals, ranging through caring for rare endangered species saved from illegal trade, rehabilitation of local injured wildlife, quarantine kennels with care of dogs and cats, animal welfare, and more.

Discovering Kwan Yin

For our first few months in Hong Kong, we stayed in a hotel close to Nathan Road in Tsim Sha Tsui, Kowloon.

Here, there were many china and porcelain shops. We had arrived in Hong Kong with just two suitcases of clothes, and no household goods. So I went to look for these, including china goods such as plates and cups. I found myself looking in these local china/porcelain shops, and in these shops I came across some beautiful statues of a wonderful lady in long robes. Her face was beautiful. She was peaceful and serene, and I was attracted to this beautiful lady. My friends told me who she was. They told me that her name was Kwan Yin (or Kwun Yam in the Cantonese dialect), and she was considered to be the Symbol of Mercy. Buying the cups got forgotten for a while as I was fascinated by Kwan Yin, and I spent time learning more about this wonderful lady. Later on, a friend bought me a beautiful statue of Kwan Yin, and this was my first statue of her.

Religions

As a child, I had been brought up Catholic, but now I started to use the concept of Buddhist-Christian as I came to understand that the great religions teach us to live better lives for the greater good of all life, and to live in peace, harmony and compassion with humans, non-human animals, and nature.

Nowadays, I teach many people of different religions and I respect all religions. In their roots the great religions have a space for animals and for peaceful compassionate living.

Settling Down in Hong Kong

But back to the story. Accommodation was provided as part of my husband's work contract, and it was not long before we were allocated an apartment on Hong Kong Island.

Soon after we moved in, some friends were leaving Hong Kong. They had two budgerigars who needed a good home. Our flat was empty without animals, so we took these two birds home. It was fun talking to these two birds as they were always optimistic and saw the world in a bright light as though the sun came up and shone every day. They loved to fly freely around the apartment.

My husband's work brought him into contact with many different animals who needed help and special care and treatment. One day, just several months after we had arrived in Hong Kong, he brought home two large white rabbits, both female, which had been abandoned in a street. They had mange, and needed care and treatment. No-one else would adopt them at that time and so they came home to our apartment. We treated them to cure the mange, and we allowed them to live free range in the apartment.

Now, rabbits seem to get a thrill from biting into live electrical wires and have a strange resilience to electricity, even though mains electricity is potentially dangerous to rabbits and can harm or kill them. Nevertheless, these two rabbits enjoyed themselves biting into and damaging several electrical wires which my husband had to repair. We solved the problem by enclosing the wires and cables in long runs of reinforced garden hose which was tough enough and tasted bad enough to prevent the rabbits from biting into it.

One day when I was in the apartment, I heard one of the rabbits say: "She is so gorgeous, I must have her" I saw the bigger of the two rabbits chasing the smaller rabbit around the apartment until they were both in the bathroom, which had green tiles on the floor, where the smaller rabbit stopped, while the larger rabbit mounted her. I heard the larger rabbit say: "You are so beautiful." Confused about their behaviour, I discovered that they were lesbians, and seemed to be madly in love with each other.

Next, we were introduced to a white tom-cat which had been abandoned and then rescued by a friend who was a committee member in the local "cat fancy" (a club of cat lovers), a cat lover. But he was not happy living in her home with her other cats there, so he moved into our apartment with us. We named him Sebastian. As a result of his former unhappy life and abandonment before he was rescued, he was sad and psychologically disturbed when he moved into our apartment. It took a lot of my animal communication skills to calm Sebastian down and to get him happily settled into our home.

This friend, through the "cat fancy", assessed this handsome white tom-cat Sebastian as being of the breed or type known as Chinese White Longhair, all white but with the two black marks on the upper forehead typical of this type or breed. When he was rescued, he had not been neutered, and the friend enthusiastically arranged for him to be the stud male to a few female cats of the same type/breed.

We are aware that there are so many homeless cats that we would not normally be involved in breeding more cats, as of course happened when Sebastian was a stud. As he belonged to our friend, we were not in control. Doubtless Sebastian enjoyed his times with the lady cats to whom he was introduced, and the several kittens which resulted all found good homes.

When the friend left Hong Kong a few years later, Sebastian retired from his stud duties and lived a quiet life with us at home in Hong Kong for many years.

A little later, another cat which someone had left behind in Hong Kong, a neutered male Tonkienese cat named Harvey, moved in to live with Sebastian in our apartment. These two boys became great friends and lived happily together with us.

Sebastian and Harvey were about the same ages as each other. Death eventually takes all of us, and Harvey was the first to die at the age of 15 years. Sebastian missed Harvey greatly. Sebastian was very unhappy and mourned the loss of Harvey. This was one of the saddest times of my life as I helped Sebastian to get over the death of Harvey. Sebastian lived another year until he too died from old age.

Soon after this, a friend of ours who was an expert in reptiles and fish was leaving Hong Kong to return to his birthplace in USA to seek his career path there, but the authorities there would not allow him to take one of his animals which was a piranha fish. So Frankenstein, as the piranha was called, came to live with us in the biggest fish tank we could find. Frankenstein lived with us until he died from old age some years later. Frankenstein used to tell me that my husband was too noisy as he thumped around the apartment.

Rosina Maria Arquati: The Life Journey of an Animal Communicator

For a few months, while Frankenstein was with us, we took care of a big fat cat while the cat's humans were away in New Zealand. Frankenstein's tank was covered by a strong flat board, and the cat loved to sit on top of this board on top of the tank. Frankenstein most certainly did not appreciate this, and he was very happy when the cat went home to his owners on their return to Hong Kong.

Pangolins are "scaly ant-eaters" which live wild in south-east Asia, and are a species which is also native to Hong Kong. They are cute harmless creatures which can thrive when left to live their lives in the wild in appropriate habitat. With such a specialized diet they are very difficult, often impossible, to keep alive and well in captivity. There are textbook diets for them, but often a wild pangolin will refuse these.

Sadly, pangolin scales and meat are considered by some people to be of medicinal value. Because of this, many pangolins have suffered badly by being caught in gin traps and other traps, so that they could be sold for their scales and meat. For freshness they would often be shipped alive, without food or water, often suffering from serious injuries caused by the traps.

Such trade has long been illegal in Hong Kong. Apart from the cruelty in the trade, these pangolins are endangered species and protected wild animals, protected by law. From time to time, attempts to intercept such illegal animal trade and cruelty were successful. The pangolins were seized and the offenders prosecuted. When possible, the pangolins would be rehabilitated and released to the wild.

One such pangolin was "Pango". Although having suffered substantial soft tissue injuries from a trap, his bones and limbs and essential organs and structures were intact. So Pango was sent to us for recovery. As usual, Pango refused all textbook diets, which would have been strange and foreign to him compared to the wild diet. Pangolins store body fat, on which they can live for a few weeks without food, and this saved Pango as well as other pangolins. So, for Pango, it was a race to help the wounds to heal so that he could be released to the wild as soon as possible.

During the few weeks healing time, Pango settled into our home. The apartment was in an old low rise building, and it was not unusual for some ants to come and go. We had several large pot plants, and ants lived in the soil in the pots. Pangolins are nocturnal, and every night Pango would wander from pot to pot, digging into the soil and presumably consuming the ants. While Pango was there, we never saw an ant. Presumably he had had them for dinner.

One morning, the part-time maid found Pango nicely curled up in a plant pot with a pile of soil to the side of the pot which he had dug up. She was used to the animals in our home and left him there in peace. Later she told me "I saw that he looked so comfortable and I did not want to disturb him, so I left the pile of soil there on the floor." Quite right too. When I went to check Pango, he told me that he had had a delicious dinner of ants the night before and needed to sleep off the meal. He felt happy and contented.

Another morning, we could not find Pango. I heard him call: "I am here with a friend, very cozy." I could feel that he was in a cupboard. So we looked in the cupboard, and Pango said "Meet my friend". He was curled around an empty box from an old whiskey bottle. "This is my friend," he said. And I replied "That's nice for you." He looked comfortable, and we left him to sleep there undisturbed through the day with his friend Johnny Walker. He had curled around the outside of the box and had gone to sleep hidden amongst other boxes in the cupboard. It looked like the morning after the night before, quite a picture, but all very sober in reality.

Pango's wounds healed quickly, and within a few weeks he was released into a forest area where there were many ants and termites.

CHAPTER 7

The Animals Keep Coming

Some two years later, we were fortunate enough to be allocated a big old house on the other side of the harbour in Kowloon as our new home, with a garden, a basement, and a real fireplace, all in downtown Kowloon. This was to be our home for the next fifteen years, and it became a place for many wonderful rescued animals for rehabilitation of some and for others to live out the rest of their lives happily. I learned many things from these animals, and they helped me to become a caring and loving animal communicator.

One Christmas, a tiny black dog was abandoned at the dog pound under an obviously false allegation that he was a dangerous biting animal. My husband was visiting the dog pound and saw this little dog. The doggy wagged his tail. It was apparent that he was not at all dangerous and my husband went into the kennel and befriended him. I went to visit this little dog, who told me that he was old and needed a good home, and he was not at all dangerous. We adopted him and took him home. We named him "Savage", though he was certainly not savage. He was an interesting little doggy with the body of a French bulldog and the head of a Chihuahua, and he had a very deep bark. His bark was so deep and loud that he proved to be a great guard dog when people heard him from the other side of a door, so long as they could not see what a little doggy he really was. Little Savage promised me that he would always protect me.

A month later, another little doggy was abandoned in the dog pound. She wagged her tail when she saw my husband. She too needed a home now, and we took her home to live with Savage. She was a young lady, just a year old, and was very very energetic and lively. She kept on telling me that girls just want to have fun. We named her Samantha. Samantha and Savage became great friends.

At that time, the formerly rabies-free Hong Kong had a problem as rabies had just entered Hong Kong. Stray dogs were getting a bad name in the hysteria about rabies, and there were calls to eliminate stray dogs which was of course a very difficult task as people continued to abandon their dogs. It was the 1980's, and the concept of what we now know as in-situ humane dog population management for stray and feral dogs without killing them was not widely known. The then head of a local animal welfare group, a somewhat outspoken gentleman whom we will call Frank (not his real name), had the notion in his head that walking a bitch in oestrus (in season, on heat) in the street would cause all the male strays to come rushing over to her and be caught. When Frank "got a bee in his bonnet", he was convinced he was right.

So it was given a try. Two unspayed abandoned bitches in the dog pound were saved, to become canine "ladies of the night". When they came into season, on heat, they were taken out for walkies, to walk the streets on a leash at midnight in areas where packs of stray dogs were known to roam. Some nights my husband was tasked with walking them. Theories are one thing, reality may be very different. Frank's notion was a failure this time. Dogs are very intelligent creatures, and the stray dogs were far too bright to fall for this trap. Naturally wary of humans, they proved too wise and instead of coming over to the bitch in heat, they ran the other way with their own pack bitches following them. By this time, all concerned in the exercise had become attached to these two canine ladies of the night, named Granny and Sophie, and they had to be saved. Frank and his organization would not help.

So they came home to us. Fortunately, the house and garden were very big with plenty of space for the now four dogs living with us and the other animals.

Nearby lived a man with a dog named Trizza. The man enjoyed a few beers at home each evening after work. Trizza lay at his feet. Feeling like he wanted to share, the man would give her some beer in a dish to drink. Some years later, he left Hong Kong, and like so many others, left the dog behind. Trizza found a home with us. When Trizza came to live with us, she was very nervous, and I spent a lot of time talking to her and telling her that she was safe with us and she did not need to worry. She remarked that she saw how happy the other dogs were in our house, and they were free to go everywhere. I told her that she could have the same fun and games with us, as she was now part of the family. I spent much time talking with Trizza and gaining her confidence and helping her to feel happy in our home. Before long, she became a happy member of our household.

Trizza was prone to bouts of ill health. Tests were not conclusive in identifying the cause, as comprehensive blood tests were not available in Hong Kong then as they are now, but she recovered each time with treatment. After a few years, however, she no longer responded to treatment as the damage to her liver from the beer given to her by her former human was too severe, and she passed away aged about 9 years. A post mortem examination was carried out, and, sure enough, she had advanced cirrhosis of the liver, a condition commonly caused by drinking too much alcohol.

The house progressively became a haven for all sorts of creatures who needed a sanctuary or rehabilitation. They all had interesting stories.

Out in a remote part of Hong Kong's Sai Kung Peninsula lived another friend in a large house and garden. She kept eight hens in her garden with a hen house for shelter, and collected the eggs they laid. The hens had been given to her by a neighbor. One of them had an old leg injury. She was able to walk pretty well, but with a limp. The limp put this hen towards the bottom of the pecking order amongst the flock of eight hens. When we visited one day, our friend asked us how the leg could be improved. My husband suggested an X-ray picture to see what was wrong with the joint which was injured. Our friend told her parents this, and they burst out laughing. They had never heard of a chicken being X-rayed, and they thought the easier solution would be to eat the chicken!

Several weeks later, there was a knock on our door. On the doorstep was this same friend holding the chicken. Inside the house, she explained: "This is the chicken that needs an X-ray of her leg. Can I leave her with you and come back in a few days after her X-ray has been done?" This was something of a surprise, but my husband agreed, and the chicken moved in for a few days.

The X-ray picture showed an old injury to the leg joint which could not be cured. However, this chicken was able to walk and run pretty well, despite her limp. So we called her human, who promised to come over. After a few weeks, she did return. As she came into our house, she said: "The place where I was living is too remote. I have left there and moved into the city area now. I have given the other seven hens to a neighbor where I was living, and I now have nowhere to keep this one."

By this time, this hen had already settled into our home. We had already named her "Hopalong", on account of her limp. She had her own quarters in the old laundry room which opened directly onto the garden, and during the daytime she would run around with all the dogs living with us. Fortunately our dogs and cats were mild and gentle and did not harm other creatures, so Hopalong was safe. She was not afraid of the dogs or cats, and acted as a member of the pack of dogs.

Early on, when I was feeding the dogs, Hopalong came running in first and said: "Get these dogs out of the way, and give me my food first."

I said to her, "I am happy to give you your food first, but please do not upset the dogs."

Her response was, "That's fine, but if the dogs get in my way, I can flutter up onto their backs and annoy them!"

Hopalong's food was entirely vegan of course.

Hopalong was, literally, a "party animal". She loved to attend parties, and would sit on people's laps and snuggle up to them. Her party trick was to demonstrate that she knew the difference between white rice and whole grain brown rice. Guests would hold a few grains of white rice in one hand, and a few grains of whole grain rice in the other hand. Hopalong would enthusiastically eat the whole grain rice from their hands, but refuse the white rice. As she ate the whole grain rice, she picked up one grain at a time rapidly pecking it from the hand. When a chicken pecks at food, it is accurate and gentle. The sharp beak was so accurately and carefully aimed at each grain that people hardly felt anything as she pecked up the grains from their hands. No sharp peck, just pure gentleness.

Hopalong was of the breed of chicken known as White Leghorn, a breed which farmers have developed to lay frequent infertile eggs without mating. Hopalong laid one egg almost every day, but, whatever religion applied to her, she kept the Sabbath! For at least her first 5 years with us, she laid one egg per day from Monday to Saturday, six days a week. On Sundays she rested. She was remarkably consistent in this, until she became too old and started to lay very few eggs. Who knows how she knew it was Sunday, except that that was the day when everyone was at home. We did know that these eggs were humanely produced by this rescued happy chicken, Hopalong.

Hopalong was about 2 years old when she came to live with us. She lived with us another 7 years. In those days, my father-in-law, who lived in London, regularly came to stay with us in Hong Kong for a holiday each

Rosina Maria Arquati: The Life Journey of an Animal Communicator

year. When he stayed with us, he was the one taking care of Hopalong, and he became very fond of her, even though he would then go out to dinner in the evening and order roast chicken.

Hopalong died peacefully in her sleep at about nine years old, quite elderly for a chicken, at a time when my father-in-law was in Hong Kong and taking care of her. He was very very upset when she died. After this, he stopped eating chicken. But his mourning only lasted a few weeks, and within a month he was back to ordering roast chicken for dinner.

Chapter 8

Many Species Need Care

Sabrina

One Saturday, soon after Hopalong had joined us, a lady was walking in the forest area commonly known as "Monkey Hill" because wild macaque monkeys live there, when she came across a day old wild monkey abandoned on the ground. Exactly why this baby monkey was so abandoned was not known then, but it is believed that when a dominant male monkey takes control of a new group of female monkeys, he may kill the babies born to other males so that his genes become more dominant in the population. This lady rushed the baby over to the aforementioned Frank at the animal welfare group, who called his vet to treat it. The organization's vet at that time felt unable to treat a monkey, and so Frank called my husband: "Dr David, a baby monkey has just been brought in to us, with no mother. What should we do?" My husband went to examine the baby. He adjudged that the baby monkey was not seriously injured and had a fair chance of recovery, but needed special care and regular feeding with suitable baby milk every few hours. Frank was unwilling and unable to take this on, but after a few telephone calls my husband was able to find another wildlife veterinarian, whom we will call Mike, who was willing to take on the job. Problem: Mike was overseas on that day.

So this baby monkey came to our home for care and feeding until Mike returned from overseas. But politics and bureaucracy seem to thrive on obstructing common sense. Wild monkeys are a protected species, and of course this baby had to be reported to the authorities in accordance with the law. By the time Mike had returned, the authorities found themselves in a dither and unable to make any decision about finding a suitable carer such as Mike to care for the baby monkey. So we were asked to take care of the baby monkey until the authorities could make a decision, a decision process which took nine months! We named her Sabrina.

So there we were with this baby monkey in our care for nine months. Sabrina was about one day old when she came to us. We cared for her, bottle feeding her every few hours, and she thrived and grew. Soon she wanted to run around and climb, and so we fitted her with a modified diaper and she was allowed to run freely around the living room when we were there.

Sabrina with me, 1980s

When my husband was away, Sabrina loved to be naughty. I would communicate that when "her daddy" came home I would tell him about her being naughty.

She always said "Daddy will never believe you, because when he comes home I will be like an angel for him."

Lo and behold, as soon as my husband arrived home, Sabrina would become his little angel. She would jump up and sit on his shoulder and look at me and say "See, he will never believe that I was naughty", as she made cooing noises into his ear.

Visitors came from time to time to our house, and Sabrina took a particular liking to two of those visitors: one a friend of Indian ethnicity, and the other a bald-headed American man. The living room had a high ceiling, and high pelmet boards above all the windows. Sabrina loved to climb the curtains, sit on the pelmets, then jump off to land on the soft padded armchair or sofa. But when either of these two visitors came, instead of jumping onto the seat, she would aim herself to land on the visitor's head or shoulder, from behind. Having a monkey suddenly land on your head would take anyone by surprise, but fortunately these folks took it in good humour and were honoured that this little monkey liked them both so much.

As Sabrina was having fun jumping, she would call out to me and say: "Mummy, I love him, I want to be near him." Before I had time to say anything, she had landed and was snuggling up to her human boyfriend.

Sabrina had no experience of life in the wild, and it was felt that attempting to release her to the wild would probably result in her being killed or being unable to find enough food. So she lived with us for nine months until, eventually, the authorities found themselves able to make a decision of sorts, and Sabrina went to live with Mike and his staff to continue her long term care.

The Kite

One day, my husband received another call from the same Frank at the animal organization. A member of the public had brought in an injured kite found on a footpath in the Central District of Hong Kong. This bird was not able to fly. These Black Kites are wild birds native to Hong Kong and many other countries. One wing had been injured. It is quite usual to see them flying over the city area as they can scavenge food disposed by restaurants and eat quite well this way. The bones and joints and feathers of this bird were intact, but a major tendon had been completely severed in one wing. Frank's in-house vet had suggested euthanasia. However, my husband was able to surgically repair the tendon and the wound. This bird needed a place to recover, and so he was brought to our house where we had a place for this.

Once the injury had fully repaired several weeks later, this bird was transferred to a large aviary in the wildlife rehabilitation centre in the New Territories where my husband worked at the time. The bird continued to make good progress and regained the ability to fly normally. After several months this kite was allowed to fly off into the wild.

Tootsie and Chirpy

A while after that, a policeman was walking along a city street in Hong Kong, when he saw a small owl flutter down and land in the street. The owl did not, could not, fly away, nor did it try to run away.

Being a conscientious caring copper, the policemen picked up the owl, and later that day the bird found its way into my husband's care. The owl, a collared scops owl, was quite old, with poor vision and a deformed wing from an injury which had apparently occurred some years earlier. It was never clear how she appeared in the street, but she must have been kept by someone for her to have survived. She could not be rehabilitated for return to the wild as her vision was not good enough, and she behaved as though she was very tame and domesticated. So she was passed to us for care. We called her "Toot Toots" because of the sounds she made, "Tootsie" for short.

When we were at home, Tootsie was free-range in the house. With poor eyesight, free range was limited for her. So her favourite place was sitting on my husband's shoulder or on my shoulder. That way she got to ride around the house on us.

Tootsie on my shoulder

A little later, a very young owl was brought to us for care, a scops owl. At first it was still necessary to hand feed this baby, but she quickly learned to eat by herself. Being a baby, she chirped rather than hooted, so we called her "Chirpy-Chips", or "Chirpy" for short.

Chirpy was given an enclosure on our balcony next to Tootsie, and they both became friends. Like Tootsie, Chirpy had free range inside the house when we were home. Once she had learned to fly indoors, her enclosure on the balcony was left open and she was free to fly away if she wanted to. She chose to stay.

Unlike Tootsie, Chirpy was young and fit. She would fly freely around the house when we were at home, and she did. But her favourite thing was to sit on the mantelpiece, perfectly still, but watching. When visitors came, she used to say to me: "I am going to sit still on the mantelpiece and look like a statue, and then I will suddenly fly across the room to surprise them!" And she did, often.

Tootsie was old, and less than 2 years later she died suddenly. As I wrote earlier, young Chirpy always had freedom to fly away if she so decided. Soon after Tootsie died, Chirpy did indeed fly away one evening into the big trees outside the house, and "left home" forever.

The Evidence Pigeons

Crime should never be allowed to succeed. One extortionist in Hong Kong decided to threaten a major company with bombing unless they paid him a large amount of money. This man had his own idea about how to do this. He arranged for several homing pigeons to be delivered to the company in a basket! With the pigeons was a note ordering the company to attach the required sums of money to the legs of the pigeons and release the pigeons so that they could fly the money home to him. The company was having none of this and rightly called in the police! In an effort to locate the man, the relevant law enforcement agency released some of the pigeons and followed them in a helicopter with the idea of following the birds home to catch the extortionist. Pigeons are very versatile flyers, and the helicopter people soon lost sight of them. So the company was still left with four pigeons and nowhere to care for them properly. Inevitably they were passed to the avian care centre where my husband worked, and they lived there for two years in an aviary there under an order that they were to be kept there because they might be needed as evidence in court.

Investigations were eventually successful in bringing the man to justice, and in due course he was convicted. With the case completed, the pigeons needed a new home. They were domestic homing pigeons, not wild birds, so release to the wild was not an appropriate option.

So, in all innocence, my husband's colleagues, took the four pigeons along to Frank hoping that his organization would be able to locate a homing pigeon fan who would adopt them and care for them. Frank's response shocked them. "Oh, they look nice," he announced, "I will send them to the old folks home for their dinner." The old folks home was not short of food, and did not need to eat these four pigeons.

After two years of caring for these birds, my husband's colleagues had become fond of the pigeons, and had no intention of letting them end up on a dinner plate. Instead, they picked up the birds and marched out from Frank's centre, and headed to us.

After keeping them in an aviary in our garden for a few weeks, the pigeons adopted our house as their new home. We had no wish to confine them forever. When we opened the aviary doors, the pigeons came to fly freely and always returned to their home with us.

Goldilocks

Goldilocks was a golden lion tamarin in a local endangered species rescue centre and zoo where she had given birth to several babies over the years. She was ten years old. Tamarins are very small "monkeys" [primates] native to central and south america. They are nowadays rare and are being saved as a species by breeding in rescue centres.

To me, tamarins are amongst the most beautiful creatures on the Earth. They have faces and fingers like little people: they have the faces of people and the fingers of people. They are so beautiful, and they remind me of the Elementals.

One Christmas morning, Goldilocks found herself in an argument with a male tamarin, and she came out of the argument with a badly bitten tail. My husband was called out and the tail was surgically repaired and bandaged. But it was itchy, and a little later she chewed the bandage off and chewed the tail.

Rosina Maria Arquati: The Life Journey of an Animal Communicator

So back my husband went and repaired the tail and applied a lighter bandage to make it less itchy, together with some medication to calm her down and reduce the itchiness. The length of tail remaining was quite short, and if she caused any more damage to the tail it would become dangerously close to the lumbar spine. Every day the bandage had to be changed to a new one. She needed observation, and so my husband would bring her home every night for observation and medication as needed, and I would talk to her.

One evening, my husband had to go to a meeting. "Could you look after Goldilocks for me please, Rosina," he asked.

"Yes, of course," I replied, "no problem."

So Goldilocks, the dogs, and I settled down for an evening of relaxation and watching television, or so I thought.

Then I heard Goldilocks say, "Has David gone out?"

"Yes", I said," he has gone to a meeting and will be back in a few hours."

The dogs and I settled down for the programmes which I wanted to watch, with Goldilocks nearby so that I could watch her.

Then I heard Goldilocks say, "My tail is a bit itchy, so I will chew the bandage off now."

I stood up and said: "No you can't!"

In telepathic empathy, the dogs seemed to chorus my thoughts, and we all told her: "No!"

She calmly looked at us, and said: "Yes, I can. Are you going to stop me?"

Shocked by her response, the dogs and I looked at each other. "What are we going to do with her?"

I told the dogs I would negotiate with her so that she would know how serious it would be if she bit her tail any more, which I did.

"You're not the vet," she responded, "so how do you know?"

"Well, David told me so," I commented.

From her: "Are you sure?"

From me: "Yes."

Then I realized that she was not going to follow my advice. So I had to page David. He promptly called back by telephone, and I also had the telephone close to Goldilocks. I told him what had been going on. As I put the phone by Goldilocks, she listened to David's voice, and I explained to her. I put down the phone.

Goldilocks looked at me: "Message received, I must not bite my tail, sorry."

The dogs looked at me: "Will she stop biting her tail?"

"Yes," I responded, "and I will give her some healing to relax her, then we should be OK for the rest of the evening."

When David arrived home, Goldilocks was happy about not biting her tail any more. After this she never bit her tail.

She could not return to her home at the centre until her tail was completely healed, until there was no more itchiness, and no more medication or bandaging needed. Seven weeks later, her now short tail was fully healed, and she was returned to her home.

When I visited her there some days after she had returned to her family and friends, Goldilocks thanked me for stopping her from biting her tail. She was happy and was back with her friends and family, and many people were talking about her unusually short tamarin tail.

Samantha the dog with myself and a young Golden Headed Lion Tamarin (not Goldilocks)

We lived in this large house for fifteen years, and while we were there, many creatures joined us for rehabilitation and care until they were returned to the wild or back to their homes, or found good new homes, or passed away from old age.

CHAPTER 9

Moving again

Gigi was a white Japanese Spitz-cross. Her humans had left Hong Kong and gone to live in England, but little Gigi was left behind with an animal welfare society. The head vet at the society called my husband, and we had space at our home for Gigi. Later that day I went to meet Gigi at the society, and the next day she came to live with us.

Buddy was a nightclubbing Shitzu. He belonged to a cabaret singer and would regularly be there at the club enjoying the show and enjoying all the fussing and petting which he attracted. But then a baby human came along and Buddy the dog was out of the picture. This was soon after Gigi had come to live with us. As we knew Buddy very well, he eventually came to live with us.

Gigi was a lady of style, sedate and well-mannered. Buddy was more of a country bumpkin, boisterous, playful and fun-loving. These two completely different individuals quickly became great friends, with Buddy frequently leading Gigi into mischief, with fun and games around the house.

We lived in the large house for fifteen years. There were six of these houses in a row. They belonged to my husband's employers, and the land was worth a lot of money. So inevitably the houses were sold off for redevelopment, and nowadays a large building containing many apartments stands there.

We closed the door for the last time on our beautiful old house. It was January. We were sad to leave as it was a wonderful place for the animals to come to, and all the wonderful memories of the animals who had passed through this house flashed back.

***

Some of the dogs, and the cats, had already died from old age by the time we left the house. The other animals had either died from old age, returned to the wild or their old homes when recovered, or found new homes. Samantha, Gigi and Buddy were getting quite old by this time, but were still with us, active and well. I explained to them that we would be living in an apartment, with a balcony. So, we all got into a taxi to our new home, Samantha, Gigi, Buddy, David and myself.

It was not long until the household of animals started to grow again.

***

Chapter 10

Baby Primates

Josh

The havoc and destruction that humans have wrought on wildlife and nature are horrendous. Mother orang-utans are wonderful mothers, caring for their youngsters for several years until the young ones are ready for independence, and protecting the youngsters from danger. Horrifically, on the island of Borneo, many wild mother orang-utans have been shot and killed by illegal poachers just to get the baby orang-utans. The babies could then be sold as pets, even though it is ridiculous and cruel to consider raising an orang-utan as a pet: they can grow to over 100 Kg.

Josh was such a sadly orphaned little baby orang-utan. He was discovered hidden down below on a cargo ship in transit which was anchored in Hong Kong waters to load and unload some cargo. As an illegally smuggled endangered species, he was rescued by the authorities, and charges laid against the seamen responsible. Caring for a motherless unweaned baby orang-utan is a thoroughly exhausting task. Josh was underweight, undernourished and starting to dehydrate. The care of Josh was immediately started by one of my husband's colleagues, with round the clock care and bottle feeding. Three days later, my husband's colleague understandably collapsed from exhaustion.

Rosina Maria Arquati: The Life Journey of an Animal Communicator

My husband, David, was on a trip overseas at this time. He arrived back to find two similarly tired staff and Josh in his office. Following the exhaustion of the first carer, Josh had been passed to David's animal care staff. We will call them Jim and John. These two male nurses had already been taking care of Josh for some days, working long shifts from early morning to late at night. The two of them became Josh's substitute human mothers for as long as Josh was with us. Josh was still a little baby, unweaned, dependent now on human love and care, with bottle feeding every few hours, nappy changing whenever he pooed, and in need of humans to cuddle him as his mother would have been doing in the jungle if poachers had not killed her. Added to this, orang-utans are so closely related to we humans that they can be susceptible to some of our diseases. Even the common cold could have devastating results for a baby orang-utan. So it was important for Jim, John, David and myself (I was of course a frequent visitor to Josh) to keep ourselves healthy and free from infectious diseases in order to protect the health of Josh.

Jim and John's efforts and long hours caring for Josh succeeded. Josh rehydrated, gained weight, and became an active healthy baby. He continued to grow, and over the ensuing months he was gradually weaned onto solid food, and onto water to drink. Now, an orang-utan can comfortably hold his own body weight hanging by one arm, so you can imagine how strong the arms of an orang-utan can be, even a young one. Josh was kind and gentle. But he was mischievous and liked to play up sometimes, like many human children do.

Josh cuddling up to me

One day, when Jim and John were out for a quick lunch, my husband decided that Josh's nappy needed to be changed. I was visiting Josh at the time. We had changed various animal nappies hundreds of times before, including monkeys. Josh decided to play games with David. Orang-utans can use their legs and feet, as well as their arms and hands, with the dexterity that we enjoy only with our arms and hands. So it is like a baby with four strong arms and four hands. As David put on the nappy, Josh would then bring up one of limbs and push it off. Again and again. Josh was having a great time teasing David like this.

After several minutes, Jim and John came back and took over. After changing Josh's nappies for weeks already, they had become very skilled at this. Josh behaved for them like an angel, and his clean nappy was on in no time at all.

Josh attracted a lot of publicity, and soon the authorities from his country of origin came to visit him. They agreed that he was an illegally smuggled baby, and arranged for him, when fully weaned and old enough to travel, to be taken to an orang-utan rehabilitation centre on Borneo, where orphaned orang-utans are rescued, integrated with other orang-utans, and taught how to survive in the wild before their eventual release.

Jim and John, however, needed a holiday.

Tom

The belief that mothering instincts come automatically is not always correct. There are times when humans and animals cannot handle a newborn, and this was the case with Tom, a newborn baby emperor tamarin. His mother had given birth to this lovely baby tamarin, but just sat there looking at the baby, with little interest and no maternal behaviour. She had no idea what to do. Tamarins are protected/endangered species, and Tom was born in a conservation centre which was part of the international breeding programme to save these animals.

After a few hours of no maternal care, it was clear that the mother had no idea what to do with this baby, with Tom just a few hours old sitting on the branch alone. It was agreed that hand rearing was the only way to save him.

Once again our home was being set up as a nursery.

"Rosina, he is a newborn, do not get too attached, he may not make it as he is very small, the size of my thumb. He will be on two-hourly bottle feeds."

I gave the little tamarin some healing and talked to him while David prepared his first baby-bottle of milk,

"What can we call him, David," I queried.

Quickly, the storybook character Tom Thumb came to mind.

"He is only as big as my thumb, so let's call him Tom Thumb."

So Tom he was.

Every day, Tom went to work with David, and every night they came home together. Day and night, Tom was bottle-fed.

Well, Tom made it, and after a few weeks he was running around the apartment. David on the other hand was exhausted. Tom had integrated into our home nicely. His favorite place was sitting on the head of myself or my husband and being carried around the house like that: What else would a baby emperor tamarin expect.

Tom in his favourite position

Our dogs at the time were coping well. I had explained to them that Tom's mother did not know how to look after him and that was why he was with us.

My dogs have always been good as I explain to them why we have animals staying.

Rosina Maria Arquati: The Life Journey of an Animal Communicator

One night, when David and I were in bed, and the dogs had settled down for the evening, I was just going off to sleep when I heard "Mum, Mum, help me, he thinks I am a horse!"

I responded, "It's alright Gigi, I'm coming."

Half awake, half asleep, I started to get out of bed. Then, Gigi came galloping into the bedroom. There was Tom sitting on Gigi's back like a jockey.

"Tom, stop that!" I ordered.

"Why," he responded, "it is such great fun, Gigi can run very fast."

"No! Tom," I re-iterated.

Gigi jumped up onto the bed, and to Gigi's great relief, Tom jumped straight onto David's head, which of course woke him up!

Gigi looked at me and asked, "Mum, when will he be going away?"

"Well," I responded, "as soon as David says he is ready to go to live with the other tamarins."

"Will that be soon?" Gigi pressed me.

I told David of Gigi's concerns and what had happened. By then, Tom had curled up in David's hair and gone to sleep as though nothing had happened. After that, I had to explain to Tom that Gigi did not like him on her back, and such behaviour by Tom was unacceptable.

A few weeks later, David told us that Tom was ready to go to join the other tamarins. Gigi looked at me with a "What a great idea" message.

From the twentieth century into the twenty-first

The year 1997 came and went. The sovereignty of Hong Kong was returned to China. By this time, the three dogs Samantha, Gigi and Buddy were well into old age.

Buddy was first to go. Before he came to live with us, he had been living in a part of the New Territories of Hong Kong where some of our human friends had been living. Three of those human friends had all developed leukaemia/leucosis, a cancer relating to the blood and lymphatic system. Whether it was background radiation from the rocks in that area, or a virus circulating there, or some other cause, was not determined. Later on, Buddy, too, developed a cancer of his lymphatic system, called lymphoma. By the time it became clinically apparent, it was already advanced. Treatment was given to Buddy but it did not cure the cancer, as such treatment failure in such cases is so often the outcome in dogs when treatment may prolong life but without being a cure.

One morning, Buddy came round to each of us in the apartment, one by one, for a brief petting. This was his final set of farewells to us, as he passed away peacefully later that day.

The next to fade was Samantha. She was 16 years old, and for fifteen of those years she had lived with us. Her kidneys were failing, and eventually treatment was no longer able to save her. She was failing, her kidneys were beyond treatment. If left, her health would get worse and worse over the coming few days or hours, with a slow death, and the humane choice now was to end it.

So David gave the injections, and euthanasia was completed for our 16 year old Samantha.

Several months later, the local dog pound, now under a new head vet, was just re-opening the adoption doors and was again starting to allow animals to be rescued and rehomed from it. The pound had been closed to adoptions for several years until then.

The new millennium had dawned, and the year 2000 had just begun. In the very first week when the rehoming started, there were six dogs waiting at the pound to be collected by an animal welfare society for rehoming. Sure enough, the society arrived as promised and took away five of the dogs to rehome. But they left the sixth doggy behind. They said: "She's too old!".

The next day, my husband and I visited the dog pound and saw her, an ageing pomeranian, still there looking sad and dejected. She had been left behind, while the others had been taken to rehome. We went into her enclosure, picked her up, and said we would adopt her. Her whole demeanor quickly changed. We put her back onto the ground and she leapt into the air like a spring lamb, with a very happy look, and she wagged and wagged her tail. So, after we had complied with all the required adoption procedures, home to our apartment she came, and quickly made herself at home. We called her "Jasmine".

Rosina Maria Arquati: The Life Journey of an Animal Communicator

A month later, a tiny old toothless white pomeranian had been abandoned in a street. Lost and forlorn, without hope, she walked up to a passing policeman. Sympathetically, the policeman picked her up. Police procedures were such that lost and abandoned dogs were normally sent to the dog pound. There, in the pound, she sat, sad and hopeless. David happened to be visiting the pound when she was there. Seeing her, he asked the management there and was told that no-one had come forward to adopt or claim her. She was too old and in visibly poor condition. She was small, old, her teeth were bad, and her legs not very good. David told the dog pound staff there and then that we could adopt her if no-one else would. At this, the old doggy leapt into the air with a look of great joy, as Jasmine had done a month earlier. The staff there didn't delay, and, after we had complied with and completed all the necessary procedures through an animal adoption society, this geriatric tiny pomeranian, toothless and wobbly on her legs, came to live with us. We named her "Jade."

So now Gigi, Jasmine and Jade were the only dogs living with us. Jasmine and Jade, were both pomeranians in their senior years. Thus began the "Aristocratic Pomeranians", as they came to be called.

CHAPTER 12

The Aristocratic Pomeranians Come Into My Life

Montage, Rosina and the Aristocratic Pomeranians

My dream has always been to have a pack of pomeranians. Perhaps in a past life I have lived with foxes and wolves. The wish to be with animals such as huskies and Pomeranians has been in my subconscious mind for years.

As I am only five foot tall, huskies were out for me as *they* would be taking me for a walk. My dream then turned to pomeranians.

Of course, all animals are wonderful. All breeds of dogs are lovely creatures, and so are mongrels. It would be wrong to only consider one breed and ignore all others. In my work and in my life I communicate with many many species and kinds of animals, and every one is important. We had rescued many mongrels over the years. But, at that time, many ageing pomeranians were being abandoned and needed new homes, and they could not find homes as people did not want to adopt older animals. So the animal rescue organizations started to send older pomeranians to us.

We have always rescued animals and never bought them. Our dogs have usually been older dogs.

Many people will not adopt older animals. This is sad. Adopting dogs and other animals in their golden years (older animals) can give these senior animals a few more years, in a happy caring home until they pass away. Pets are for life. An older animal is good for people who, for whatever reasons, work or personal, would find it difficult to commit to up to twenty years caring for a puppy or kitten as he/she grows older.

Older dogs do not need as much exercise as young dogs, which means that long walks are not so necessary; and, because they sleep more, they are often a lot quieter than younger dogs, which can make older dogs better in flats and for working owners.

With older dogs, their characters have formed, so you know the temperament of the dog when you get him or her. On the whole, older dogs will normally have got over the problem stage of high susceptibility to puppy infections. Regular trips to the doggie groomers for a wash and blow-dry make them feel and look good. As with puppies, some may need a special diet, but most pet food companies have them readily available. House-training can be done, showing the older dog the position of his or her new toilet. It may take a little time but they can get it.

As an animal communicator, before we bring home a new animal, we will have a "family meeting". The first person to convince about bringing home a new animal is my husband and usually he says, "I say nothing."

Then I sit down with our animals and explain why we are taking on the new one. In some cases the animal is old and needs a place for the rest of his/her life. In other cases the animal might be rescued from a puppy mill (puppy farm) or other such place, and needs a home to learn and play, to be free, and to experience happiness. I explain this to the existing animals in our home and remind them what life was like before they came to live with us, and how important it is to make the newly rescued animal(s) feel at home as quickly as possible. For a new dog, I normally ask the older dogs to teach the new dog the house rules regarding toilet, meal times and relevant information.

Where possible, when adopting a new dog, we will take our current dogs to the shelter to pick up the new dog and bring him/her home.

So, when adopting dogs, our custom was that we rescued old dogs.

Jasmine and Jade were the first two of the Aristocratic Pomeranians, and have since been followed by a succession of mostly geriatric Pomeranians, which people have abandoned before they were rescued and came to live with us.

Jasmine

In the previous chapter I described how Jasmine was rejected by an animal adoption society because she was too old, and so she came to live with us. We called her Lady Jasmine.

Jade

A month later, an equally old abandoned Pomeranian walked up to a policeman in the street, but no-one would adopt such an old dog and so she too came to live with us. I named her Lady Jade.

Jasper

It was not long after this when the animal rescue centre called, They had a male Pomeranian which had been returned to them three times. "We cannot find a home for him; he is 8 years old, are you interested?" they said. I was heading down to New Zealand the next day, but I said that I would pop in and see him. That was it: if he did not get a home while I was away, I would take him on my return. While driving in New Zealand, I kept singing the old rugby song "Oh Sir Jasper", much to my husband's annoyance.

On our return, the boy Pomeranian was still homeless. Gigi and Jasmine and Jade were living with us, and the new boy dog would be coming to share their home with us. So off we went to get him, taking Gigi, Jade and Jasmine with us to collect the dog. Gigi refused to enter the building as this was the same place from whence she herself had been rescued some ten years earlier. But we told her that it was all right and we would not leave her, and continued to reassure her that it was OK and we were just getting a new dog.

When we rescue a new dog we try to take the existing dogs with us to get the new dog. The existing dogs then know where the new dog has come from, and it is a lot easier for the new dog to be accepted into the pack. (The old dogs still remember the dog rescue kennels only too well.) I named our new dog Sir Jasper, not after the rugby song, but after the gemstone jasper.

Jasper's lower teeth looked like fangs and so we nick-named him our Fu Dog. Now the search was on to buy a traffic cone for our young man to use as his personal post to cock his leg.

Jasmine and Gigi, their final months

Jasmine became sick from breast cancer which had spread into the lungs (metastasized); and shortly after Sir Jasper came to us, Jasmine left the planet in a way I will never forget. When my animals have to leave the planet, they normally do so at home. Over the years we have considered the needs of animals and owners when this time comes, and we apply this to our own animals. Jasmine said good-bye to Gigi, Jasper and Jade, and came into the room we had set up for her. She knew that it was time to go. I gave her some Reiki and kissed her. She sat by my husband as she was his dog, and looked into his eyes as if to say it was time. The vet gave her the injection and Jasmine left the planet calmly.

We let the surviving animals pay their last respects to the animal that has passed away, as they then know that their friend has moved on. We learned this when Harvey our cat died from old age: our other cat Sebastian was not there at that time as he was at the vet's, and when Sebastian came home and could not find Harvey he seemed to mourn right up until his own death from old age a year or so later.

Not long after Jasmine passed away, Gigi also passed away. Gigi was around 20 years old and a real lady.

Amber

It was not long after when I was contacted about a small pomeranian who looked young but was old, and would not be easy to re-home. I was invited to the animal rescue centre and met the dog. Yes, she was mine and I called her Lady Amber.

Lady Amber, a tiny ageing Pomeranian was adopted as a very old rescue dog in 2003. Before she came home to us, she suffered an adverse reaction to the anesthesia during her spay operation and went into a coma. Reiki alongside veterinary care helped her to recover from that.

She went on to become a happy and active elderly dog. Lady Amber always opened her heart to help other rescued dogs which joined our household.

Lady Amber lived to an estimated age of 16 to 18 years when she passed away.

Topaz

A few months before Christmas, Lady Jade, Lady Amber, Sir Jasper, and my husband and I were on a dog rescue walk. While having lunch in Lan Kwai Fong after the dog walk, I noticed another boy pomeranian. He was with his foster parents and needed a home. He looked wild and very foxy. As I walked away I found myself looking back at him. He seemed to stay in my mind. When it came to Christmas my husband asked me what I wanted, and I just said: "Let's rescue the wild and foxy doggy I met on the dog walk if he has not found a home."

I telephoned the animal rescue centre. No, he had not been re-homed. So Lady Jade, Lady Amber, Sir Jasper, my husband and I all went off to get Sir Topaz.

Now the search was on again to buy more traffic cones as we now had two boys. Our house was full with four rescued dogs and two rescued turtles.

Ammonite

Then, one day while I was having lunch with a friend, there was a phone call. An old, small, hairless female Pomeranian was looking for a home. Could I take her, I was asked, or did I know anybody who could adopt her.

If not, she was going to be put to sleep the next day. Off I went. What could I do? I already had a full house, so I said that I would foster her. But on getting her home, she quickly won the heart of my maid, and my husband knew that we would end up keeping her. We named her Lady Ammonite, after the fossil.

Smokey Quartz

Once again, I heard that a Pomeranian needed to be fostered and I agreed to foster the dog. But, while on the phone, I was asked to foster a very young puppy which was very very sick. So I agreed to take him, knowing that I had a full support team at home and that we could handle a sick pup. I brought home what my friends described as a little rat, and set up an isolation ward for him. There were supposedly going to be numerous people who were going to adopt this small puppy when his health improved. With good veterinary care, Reiki and animal communication, the young puppy pulled through: a very strong-willed young puppy I might add. And then it became time to find a new home for this puppy, whom we called Master Smokey Quartz. Prospective adopters came to see him, and whatever they wanted to see in a young puppy to be adopted, he would do the opposite. If they wanted a quiet dog, he would bark. If they wanted a lively dog, he would 'play dead'. It was soon made apparent to us that he had decided to stay. My job then was to communicate with the other dogs as to whether he could come and stay in the family, and to convince my husband that I could take a puppy. To my surprise, the female dogs, Jade, Amber and Ammonite, told me "Don't keep him," and that they would have nothing to do with 'that brat'. Jasper and Topaz said that it would be OK, but I needed to negotiate with them if they would help me to bring up that, at that stage, helpless looking pup. Much to my surprise, the boys said that they would help me.

The next person to convince was my husband, who carefully pointed out the pros and cons of a puppy, but who agreed as he always would.

So this little doggy, Master Smokey Quartz became part of the Aristocratic Pomeranians. He would not become 'Sir' until he reached the maturity of five years of age. And Master Smokey Quartz has taken over our lives.

My beloved Jade died. She was very old by this time and died peacefully in her sleep. This little dog, that gave me strength to keep going with my work, showed that however small or decrepit you are, just keep going.

Sugilite

Not long after the death of Jade, another small white 'decrepit' pomeranian appeared at the animal shelter, and once again I took her home. We called her Lady Sugilite.

Moonstone

At this time we lived with six animals, and I had made a decision 'no more dogs', due to changes in our lives. But we were invited to a party at an animal shelter. On arrival, a beautiful pomeranian went to chat up my husband. Then she found me and stayed with me for over 4 hours, knowing that I would not leave her at the shelter. And of course we took her home. We called her Lady Moonstone. She had been a breeding bitch. Going for walks and to restaurants were new experiences for her. She soon became a loving member of our family.

Many changes took place in our lives, and we and the Aristocratic Pomeranians moved to the New Territories. They no longer lived in yuppie Mid-Levels, but now became country bumpkins.

Emerald

As our lives changed, I felt that our dogs were enough. But then came another telephone call from an animal shelter. "An old pomeranian needs a home. We have tried to re-home her, but we can't. Can you take her?"

Again I heard the words coming from my mouth: "I can foster her". "OK," came the reply from the shelter. "I'll be in your area next week, so I'll drop her off." So then, Lady Emerald joined the family.

Malachite

Not long after Emerald's arrival, another shelter emailed: "I have a small old boy Pomeranian." I asked: "How old?" "About 15," came the answer. "Can you adopt or foster him?" Again, I said that I could only foster. But I was leaving for a trip, and could only take him on my return. "If he's still there, I'll come and pick him up." And, once again, on my return, I went to pick up the ageing Pomeranian. His eyesight was not so good, he liked to be the 'only' dog, and wanted lots of fuss. Integrating him would be 'fun.' So, home I went with Sir Malachite.

Opalite

I thought that my home was complete! But, just as I was leaving to go to England for a workshop, an email came through: "Do you have space for a small geriatric pomeranian? She has a skin problem, which is treatable, so will you be able to manage that?" "Well," I responded, "let me talk to the rest of the household." Silence came over the household. The dogs had given up saying "No", as had my husband. Our house was a home for geriatric animals, so one more would fit in. Thus came Lady Opalite to our house.

Lady Opalite was a tiny ageing pomeranian, when we adopted her from a rescue organization. After she came to us, we realized that she had come from an unsatisfactory environment, as a puppy farm dog, and was in very bad condition. She had been saved through a rescue group to a foster family and given veterinary care to start her way back to health, and then eventually came to us. With excellent veterinary care, she recovered to optimum health as far as possible for an old dog. She became part of the Aristocratic Pomeranians and taught us all how to send and give love no matter how others have treated us. She opened her heart to humans even though she had been badly hurt by humans in the past. Lady Opalite always opened her heart to people, and showed love to all that she met. Lady Opalite and the LOVE to and from her will always be in our hearts as a gift from her to the whole family.

Selenite

One morning I opened my email, and there it said: "Rosina, we have an old Pomeranian, in a group of dogs abandoned by a breeder. Can you take her?" I took a deep breath. My head told me that we had a full house. I looked at a photo of this dog. She was in a kennel with a younger dog. Her condition was bad.

I did not answer the email, as I needed to think, and to talk to my husband.

Much later in the evening I received a telephone call. "Did you receive the email?" Again my head said, "Full house". I explained to the animal shelter, but said that if no-one else would take her, we would come to see her. The next day she was booked for her spay operation and to start treatment for her skin and leg problem. A volunteer at the animal shelter would call me to let me know the progress.

Next day, she called me. The dog had been spayed and had had some lumps removed; and she had an old injury to her left hind leg so she walked on three legs.

The next day we visited her at the shelter. There she was: a little old lady in a kennel with a young hairless boy. She was frightened and nervous, and the two of them sat close together. I talked to her and fussed her. The young male dog had a fosterer lined up, but she had none. We would collect her two days later.

The day came. It was the day when the Aristocratic Pomeranians were going to the groomer, their "hairdresser". A day at the hairdresser for the

Rosina Maria Arquati: The Life Journey of an Animal Communicator

Aristocratic Pomeranians is an adventure, with a long trip in a van to get there.

With our other dogs settled in at their hairdresser, we went to the rescue centre. There she sat, all alone. She saw me. She got up. She wagged her tail, remembering that I had told her I would not leave her. She came to my arms and she was ready to leave the rescue centre.

We took her to the groomer, and stayed while she was shampooed because she was still rather delicate from the operation three days earlier. It seemed to be the first time she had been groomed so gently and with such attention.

Now with the other pomeranians there around her at the groomer, she perked up. She became a very different old lady: confident, running around on three legs, and joining in with the Aristocratic Pomeranians.

That evening, back at our home, she was to be kept initially in a pen for treatment of her skin condition. In the pen, she stared forlornly at the other dogs, sad and lonely again. She wanted to join in and sleep with the other dogs. So down with the pen, and out she came to join the others. Happy again. We called her Lady Selenite. At the house, Lady Selenite soon came to act as though she had been here all her life. Sir Smokey Quartz became her friend and ally as she learned about her new found freedom and how to enjoy life.

In September 2009, as I was checking-in at the City Check-in, Central, on my way to England to see my mother who was in hospital, my husband phoned me to tell me that Lady Emerald had passed away.

She had been sleeping all night on the bed with Lady Opalite and got up the next morning looking happy and alert for a senior citizen. Later that morning, my husband found her curled up and looking as if she was asleep. He went over to check as he knew that something was not right. Lady Emerald had passed away while sleeping, peacefully and painlessly.

I left Hong Kong again late on 23rd Dec 2009, leaving all my dogs in the excellent care of Michael at our home over the Christmas time, although it is always difficult for me to be away from them over Christmas. However, when I arrived in London on Christmas Eve, a text message was awaiting me saying that Lady Opalite has been rushed to the veterinary hospital and was on oxygen.

Then, on the next day, the Christmas day, 25th Dec 2009 at about 6:30am, Hong Kong Time, Lady Opalite passed away with estimated age 15 to 18 years old.

My beautiful "foo dog" Sir Jasper left the planet on 24th February 2010, aged about 20. Jasper had been with us for 10 years after having been given up by three other people before we adopted him at around 10 years of age. His unusual prance and his two fang-teeth gave him a very special appearance. He was an individual with his very own character who filled my life with love and understanding. No words can describe the love Jasper and I shared, which could only be felt with our hearts. Jasper will be loved forever, and will always be remembered and missed.

Sodalite

It happened again. A little old Pomeranian needed a home. The animal shelter phoned. So, off I went to meet this old lady. She was about 14 years old and rather growsy. Her teeth were in need of treatment and she was coughing. After she had gone through some initial veterinary treatment, we took her home. She was more ill than we had been told, and she was not eating. And she didn't like the other dogs. Smokey Quartz went to greet her, and she growled at him. "Keep that dog away from me", she said. Then on Monday, I gave her healing: by the afternoon, she started eating, and soon she was joyfully running around together with the group of Aristocratic Pomeranians, and looked like she had been living happily with the Aristocratic Pomeranians for a number of years. We named her Lady Sodalite.

Each of the old dogs gradually passed away over the years as a result of their old ages

So now we had two small Pomeranians: Sir Smokey Quartz, and the then 17 year old Sir Malachite.

Strawberry Quartz

I was not going to take any more dogs. However, I was taking an animal communication workshop, and one of my students was helping out at a rescue centre where, she told me, there was a little white lady pomeranian, seven years old, in urgent need of a home.

I was in a dilemma because I was leaving for London a few days later, but my husband had just returned from Shanghai. I talked to the little girl by animal communication and knew she was very very sweet and gentle, so I sent my husband to meet her, and she was to join us. So it was a rush to bring her home, as the only day I could collect her was the day I was leaving to go to the airport.

So now we had the newest member of the Aristocratic Pomeranians: Lady Strawberry Quartz [her new name]. On the first day she did not eat so I had to ask her to eat. As soon as I had so asked, she went to eat her doggy food. She is a very pretty white senior lady pomeranian, and has thoroughly settled in with Sir Smokey Quartz and Sir Malachite.

2012: Rosina with Sir Malachite (at 18 yrs old, on lap), Sir Smokey Quartz, Lady Strawberry Quartz, and St Francis (statue)

It is the year 2013 as I finish writing this. We continue to live with our rescued animals. When I am out with them I am constantly told how beautiful my dogs look; and I am asked are they brothers and sisters, where did I get them, were they expensive, and where did I buy them. I answer that they were all abandoned dogs who have been rescued.

And, as they pass by, the Aristocratic Pomeranians hold their heads up high, knowing that they are loved.

CHAPTER 13

Animal Communication Grows

The story now returns to the latter years of the twentieth century. Keeping pets was becoming very much more popular in Hong Kong, and I was in increasing demand as an animal communicator, mainly among my friends. On one occasion, a friend insisted on giving me a red lai see packet to thank me for the animal communication sessions with her dog. After this, many people started to give me lai see packets in appreciation of my animal communication sessions. My animal communication evolved naturally, from something which I just did, into a full time professional activity. That began my career as a professional animal communicator. Still now, I ask my clients to put the money into a lai see packet, and I leave it first with my Kwan Yin at home to be blessed before I take it to the bank.

I continued with animal communication sessions for people and their pets. Gradually I developed a good reputation, and people came to me. For decades, people had told me, "No, Rosina, that is not something you can do for a living." Except, that is, for one friend some 30 years ago: after I had completed an animal communication session for her dog. She said, "You really should be doing this professionally and charging for your time, Rosina." We looked at each other, then both burst out laughing. It seemed such an unlikely career at that time. But now, years later, her idea was turning out to be true, and I was progressing in my journey as a professional animal communicator.

Rosina Maria Arquati: The Life Journey of an Animal Communicator

Then, in the year 2000, a young friend asked me to teach her animal communication. She had read some books about animal communication, and had tried to learn from the books, but could not successfully learn it from books. Could I help her? Could I teach her to be an animal communicator? I put together a workshop and curriculum to teach her how to become an animal communicator, looking at what we could do and for the best ways to get her connected to the animal kingdom. I worked out simple ways to teach her. I believe in making things simple so that everyone can learn. So I taught her the skills. She was my first student. She was amazed. She really became connected, and is now herself a very good animal communicator.

Her brother observed as she was becoming connected to the animal kingdom and getting the answers right. He was very impressed. Before long, her brother and a number of friends asked me to teach them how to communicate with animals, and my first animal communication workshop was born.

In the early years there was a lot of negativity about animal communication coming from the many people who did not believe in this. Attendance was erratic, and I worked in various places where we could find a space to hold a workshop. But it was not long before people saw the benefits of animal communication and the classes started to grow.

From these gradual beginnings, things moved ahead, and the Universe opened its doors. People were asking me to carry out animal communication sessions for their pets, and wanting me to set up workshops where they could learn animal communication. I would conduct classes and workshops when and where we could get a class up and running. I was working in Hong Kong with people from many walks of life and of various ages, though mostly the younger generation of Chinese people, all loving their pets and wanting to communicate with them. This gave me the energy to keep on going.

Rosina Maria Arquati: The Life Journey of an Animal Communicator

In time, a more permanent venue became available, and God opened all the doors. I further structured my workshops, and began to run them on a permanent basis. To encourage my students to practise regularly, I started regular students' nights. It was during one of those students' nights that we were "brainstorming" as to what more we could do with our animal communication skills to further help animals. We agreed to take the then forthcoming opportunity of World Animal Day, October 4th, to set up our first fundraiser for charity. As a group, we adopted the appellation of the Alliance of Animal Communicators Caring About Animals, AACCA.

We contacted a pet centre, and asked if they could provide some space where we could use animal communication to fundraise for some of the local animal charities. They agreed, and we went into action, getting together information, contacting local animal welfare groups, and getting set up for our first event. This was our first formal animal communication charity fundraiser event in Hong Kong. We did not know what the response would be. Donation boxes for each of the animal welfare groups were placed by each group of animal communicators so that the people could donate to the animal charities. Then we looked out of the window. People were queuing with their pets, the line was getting longer and longer and longer. Our team members were wondering what they had let themselves in for. We formed a circle, held hands, and I led a short meditation with the team. When we had completed the meditation, everyone was calm, and the energy in the room was released.

We did not have enough space indoors, so we went outside to give a brief introduction to animal communication. Then we opened the doors. The pets with their humans flowed in smoothly, and we went into action.

This became the first event of many. AACCA has become a regular part of local animal charity fundraising events, and the members of my team give up their personal time. Under the guidance of our coordinator, they provide animal communication sessions to raise funds for needy animals.

Rosina Maria Arquati: The Life Journey of an Animal Communicator

This has now expanded beyond the borders of Hong Kong. In each country where I teach, my students form a team to carry out animal communication sessions at animal charity fundraising events: in Singapore, Taiwan, Malaysia, as well as in Hong Kong.

Animal communication is my life journey. It is something which I love and enjoy doing, communicating with animals, and teaching people the skills of animal communication and connecting with their animals. This is a journey on which I am still continuing, and I do not know where it will take me in the future.

I have now been teaching regularly for over 12 years, and have students from many parts of the world. Animal communication has expanded in Asia, and my workshops give me a platform to teach people about animal welfare as well as animal communication. I love to watch my students grow and expand their skills in communicating with animals. I have students of all ages, from many walks of life, with a variety of religious beliefs. For me as a teacher I feel that it is all worthwhile to save even one animal by better understanding.

Chapter 14

Life is a Circle

Castles in Italy

In this book I started my life story with my maternal grandfather, so it is fitting that I finish the life story with my recent visit, in the summer of 2012, to "my ancestral castle" in Italy which carries my family name, Castri Arquati / Castell' Arquato. It is in Northern Italy, on a hill in the wine region. This area is a historical area of Italy with many castles nestled amidst many vineyards.

During our visit to the "ancestral family castle" of centuries ago, my husband and I decided to visit some other local castles. At one of those castles, walking through the castle grounds, we passed a small ristorante [restaurant]. As we passed, I mentioned to my husband that I would love a double espresso. We continued our exploration.

As we walked past that same ristorante, on our way back to the car, I heard, "Hi, would you like a cup of coffee? I heard you say on your way past that you would like a coffee. We are open." I looked round and saw a corgi. "They are busy at the moment as we have a big function tonight, but I will go and find someone." He went into the ristorante and returned with the ristorante owner who spoke a little English, and we ordered our double espressos. As we drank the coffee at a table outside the ristorante, the dog sat and chatted to us. He told us, "The coffee is good," and I said, "Yes, but now we have to go." He said that he would like to see us again. I said that we would like that, and I thanked him for the time that he had spent chatting with us.

Naming Dog

A few months later, visiting my mother in London, during her weekly visit to her local Methodist centre for elderly people, I found myself in their shop. While chatting with the shop manager, who knew that I talk to animals, he told me about something which happened there a few days earlier. A small boy had come into the shop with his dog. The small boy and his dog had looked around the shop to see if there was anything that they might want to buy. The boy then went over to speak to the shop manager.

"Do you know about God?" asked the boy.
"Yes," said the shop manager.
The boy continued: "Did you know that God went round giving names to all the animals, with a small puppy running after him? God went round to give names to all the animals, from Aardvark to Zebra. The little puppy was getting worried, as he thought that God would run out of names and he and his species would have no name. The puppy tried hard to get God's attention, as God was busy naming all the animals. Eventually the puppy ran in circles around God, saying 'What's my name, God, what's my name?' God said, 'It's alright. I have a very special name for you and your species, so do not worry.' The puppy got very excited, but he knew that he had to be patient and wait for God to name all the other animals. The puppy sat down and waited for God to come to him when he had finished naming all the other animals. Then, God came over to the puppy and bent over him and said, 'Your name will be my name spelt backwards: dog.' The puppy smiled and thanked God for his name, 'dog.'"

Rosina Maria Arquati: The Life Journey of an Animal Communicator

As soon as the boy had finished the story, he said "Good-bye" to the shop manager and left the shop.

The shop manager was a little surprised and bewildered by all this, and wondered why the boy had told him this story. I smiled at the shop manager: "You were told this story so that I could pass it on."

Continuing the Journey

As I finish writing this story, it is summertime in 2013, and we have three rescued doggies living with us in the New Territories of Hong Kong: the very elderly Sir Malachite, together with Sir Smokey Quartz and Lady Strawberry Quartz.

My life journey as an animal communicator continues: fascinating, heartwarming, and a wonderful experience. I continue along this wonderful journey as I continue with my animal communication work; and I continue to teach and to watch my students begin their lives as animal communicators and progressively improve their skills.

Namaste,
Rosina

PART II
Foundations of Animal Communication

Chapter 16

Introducing Animal Communication

Animals provide us with one of the best educations we can ever have in life. Animal Communication uses telepathy to communicate with animals, creating a deeper bond and understanding between humans and animals, providing us with the balance many of us require in our lives.

Animals communicate with each other via telepathy, as well as body language and vocalization and other ways (chapter 27), using the transmission of feelings, intentions, thoughts, mental images, emotions and sensations. All humans were born telepathic but, with the changes in society, complex verbal and written language has become the main human tool for communication. However, we can be taught animal communication and how to tune in and perceive what the animals are telling us.

If you have ever thought that you heard your pet "say" something to you, you could be right! Animals are able to communicate with humans who are open to the connection. They understand your intentions, emotions, images, thoughts, tones behind your words—even if they can't fully understand all the words used.

Anyone can learn animal communication; it is simple, but it does require persistence and practice. You need to put aside your mind barriers and discard any attitude of thinking that animals are less intelligent than us. Move forward with your love for animals and a willingness to learn to connect with animals.

Evolution and Basics

To make it very simple for people to understand animal communication, I try to bring it into the modern world in which we live.

Humans have evolved over many generations, and, during that evolvement, various parts of the body and mind were closed down. Humans began to domesticate animals thousands of years ago, as well as beginning early farming of plants (crops).

Humans *[Homo sapiens]* adopted friendly canids such as wolf cubs, *[Canis lupus]* into their communities. These canids/wolves adopted humans; and these wolves evolved into early "domestic dogs", including Asian dingoes *[Canis lupus dingo* or *Canis dingo]* which also travelled to Australasia probably with early humans. Humans and canids lived together and co-operated. As time moved on, the canids evolved into early 'modern' domestic dogs *[Canis lupus familiaris / Canis familiaris]*. We largely forgot the Asian dingo which continued as a wild canid. Now, the Asian dingo is a threatened species/subspecies which needs our protection.

I don't believe we ever domesticated the cat. More probably, it was a working relationship. Cats came into our communities. They kept the rodents away to protect our grains and other foods, and we would feed the cats. Scientists generally believe that the modern domestic cat [*Felis sylvestris catus* or *Felis catus*] originated from the Near Eastern wild cat, also called the Eastern Mediterranean cat or various other common names, with scientific name *Felis sylvestris lybica* or *Felis lybica*. Cats kept their sense of individuality,

Rosina Maria Arquati: The Life Journey of an Animal Communicator

and continue to keep their individuality and their "superiority" as to who they are, even till today.

"Man's best friend" [as dogs are often called in the English language], the dog, was probably "domesticated" in our early stages of evolution, before modern complex spoken and written language had fully developed; but we did have basic sounds and tones, basic vocalizations, and we did have body language; and we still had some of our telepathic skills open, so that we could also interact with the early dogs through thoughts and mind patterns.

Now our animal companions continue to have their telepathic skills open. I liken it to the modern day Skype. But most humans have closed this down through the generations of becoming increasingly dependent on written and spoken words, and, now, on computers. Scientists are still questioning where the telepathic skills are located in the brain, but we know that we do have them and our brain is like a very complex computer.

So, over the generations, most human brains have closed down their telepathic skills to the animal kingdom, but the animals still have their telepathic skills open, just like an open Skype. Every day, we have thousands of thoughts going through our brains and our animals can come in and pick up those thoughts, just like an opened Skype, but we are unable to click into their Skype system.

Language

You will see that I sometimes describe communications by writing them in a form like human dialogue, for example, "Yes," said the dog. This is to make it easier for readers to understand the communications. In reality the communications took place in the ways outlined in the following chapters. An experienced animal communicator receives messages and understands them much as he/she would understand conversation received from another human. It can be difficult for the human newcomer to understand this

Rosina Maria Arquati: The Life Journey of an Animal Communicator

concept, after years of relying on spoken and written human words. Put aside preconceptions and indoctrination, and have an open mind.

If you have ever learned a foreign [human] language, do you remember how at first you stuttered your way through the words, translating each word from your native language in your head before speaking it, and how difficult it was for you to try to comprehend the replies in the foreign language?

Then, do you remember that day when you first found yourself speaking in the foreign language without consciously translating the words or meanings in your head, when you first began to "automatically" understand the meaning in both the foreign language and your mother tongue without conscious translation? For most people that took a lot of practice time and learning time to reach that stage of "fluency" in the new language being learned, as well as time spent communicating with native speakers of the new language which you were learning?

Understanding this concept can help you understand the concept of animal communication. You will be learning a new language, new to you. To many humans, animal communication starts as a foreign language, even a strange concept, until, hopefully, with effort and practice, you can achieve a level of fluency in the art and reality of animal communication.

Learning animal communication, to become proficient in it, will need practice and on-going learning, as well as spending time with animals to understand them better.

Our "computer" brain

Now, animal communication, for youngsters, is easy to explain. Our brain is a "computer" and we can learn how to download a program to connect us to the animal kingdom so that we can click into a two-way Skype system.

Rosina Maria Arquati: The Life Journey of an Animal Communicator

Once we learn how to open up our brain, our "computer-brain", to the animal kingdom, it becomes a matter of turning it on when we want to talk with animals.

Most of us use Skype or WhatsApp, etc, and we just know that we can turn on our computer or smartphone and connect with friends by pressing a few buttons and making a few clicks here and there; we don't know the intricate details of how it operates, but we do know that it does work, and that it is very scientific. This concept helps us to understand what our brains do when we click into the world of animal communication: we are just setting up the appropriate parts of the brain to connect with the animals.

What is Animal Communication?

Animal communication is a two-way conversation. Animal communication is about receiving information that the animal knows and is passing on to the animal communicator. Animal communication should not be confused with psychics. If you go to a psychic you probably want them to predict the future, not tell you what their favorite food is and where they like to go for walks and where they like to sleep.

Animal communication can be considered like a two-way telephone link, internet service, Skype service, to the animal kingdom, sending messages to the animals by asking them about their everyday life and feelings, so that you can better understand the animals and their feelings and communications.

I try to make my workshops simple. I don't believe in making anything unnecessarily complicated. Everything is just a step by step process, just like when you download a programme in your computer. You see those little boxes appear to tell you that it has been downloaded. An animal communication workshop is basically the same. We are getting our brain computer downloaded with the right programme, so that we can click on our "PC" and connect to the animal kingdom. It is a stage by stage process and if the download is done correctly the person will be able to use the programme easily. But, like most things, when you have a new programme you need to practise.

Once you get started with your programme or workshop/training for animal communication, you do need to practise, and, as you practise being an animal communicator, you become more proficient at what you do and it becomes easier.

Feelings and Emotions, Compassion

Being an animal communicator opens you up to a very different world. It brings you to understand that animals have feelings and emotions. They are just like you and me. They have good days and bad days.

They also pick up the feelings and emotions of their humans, and that is very important to remember. I always tell people that if they want happy healthy pets, they need to do their best to be happy and healthy too. The animals which live with us become our children, our partners, our best friends, our confidants. And the world that you open up to as an animal communicator is very vast.

You have to remember that once you open up, you are connected to all sentient beings, that is, all the creatures on God's Earth; and you become much more sensitive to animals' feelings, pains and emotions, which makes it very hard for you to eat these sensitive wonderful animals. So many animal communicators will progress to become vegetarian or even vegan.

Chapter 17

Basic Concepts

You need to spend time with animals and with nature, and come to understand that animals have feelings and emotions as we do.

Spend as much time as you can in nature, and getting in touch with your inner self.

Spend time with animals when you can. You may be able to spend time with animals working in a rescue centre, or in some other situation to help animals. By being with animals, you can come to better understand them.

Animals are individuals. Each animal is different from another animal, just as you are different from another human.

Come to understand that animals are our equals and our teachers.

In some respects animals are our superiors: their forgiving natures, their unconditional love, their ability to sense illness and disease in people, their patience. Spend some time pondering on these matters.

Some animals are greatly superior to us in their senses, whether it be smell [dogs and others], hearing [dogs and others], sight [eg eagles], night vision [cats, owls, and others], and other senses. Think about this. They see, hear and smell things of which you are unaware. Some animals have senses which we lack: some fishes have electrical activity sensors which we do not have [eg the lateral line of fishes].

Come to understand that we humans are part of nature and that we cannot continue to live as if we are different from animals and apart from nature. We cannot live for long without oxygen, without water, without food, without the gravity of Mother Earth. We share these needs with other creatures on the planet. When we harm nature, when we harm animals, then we harm ourselves, our souls, and our life support system.

Chapter 18

Experience animals and nature

Daytime

For three consecutive days, visit a park, or an open wooded area, some place where you can find nature, and spend a minimum of one hour there each day.

Go there free from machines: no mobile phone, no computer. If you take your machines, you will be tempted to answer your mobile phone, check your messages. So don't take the machines.

It is OK to take a pen and notebook to jot down your observations and experiences. But you do not need to write them down if you prefer not to. Experience, observe, understand, open your mind, remember.

Spend time experiencing what is going on there. Experience and learn, but do no harm.

Open your mind and open your senses.

Look at the trees, the flowers, the grasses, the birds, the insects, the other wild creatures in nature, everything. Observe what is going on. What do you see?

Rosina Maria Arquati: The Life Journey of an Animal Communicator

Experience the smells of nature: the flowers, the grass, the park, the shrubs, the earth, the trees, the wild creatures. What do you smell?

Listen to the sounds of nature: the birds, the insects, the rustling of the wind through the trees. What do you hear?

If you are in a park or place where dogs are walking, observe how the dogs and humans interact, observe how the dogs are walking and what they are doing. What do you observe?

If you see cats there, look at how they behave, what they are doing. What do you see?

Use your senses and enhance your sensitivities: sight, hearing, smell, touch, balance, maybe taste too. And think about your less well understood senses such as telepathy. Whether or not you understand it, do you sense communication of some kind or kinds from the animals, from nature? Are you able to feel a oneness with nature and with all creatures? What do you sense? What do you feel? What do you experience?

If you have a pet, try taking your pet with you too. How does he or she react? Does he or she appear to sense things of which you are not aware?

It is important to carry out this exercise for at least 3 consecutive days. Three consecutive days is the minimum. More often and on a regular basis is better still.

Children who have grown up with animals in a compassionate environment, walking their dogs on a regular basis, living in harmony with cats, rabbits, other animals, tend to begin their connections with animals earlier and more easily.

Likewise, adults who adopt a compassionate lifestyle and enjoy walking their dogs in open spaces and being with their animals usually find it easier to connect with animals.

Night-time

On a clear night, when the skies are clear and you can see the stars, go out into an open space away from light pollution and other pollution.

Do this for a minimum of three consecutive nights. No machines, no mobile phones, no computer.

Look up at the stars. Look at the night sky, the different stars, the moon, the milky way, and other celestial bodies in the night sky if you see any [comets, shooting stars, planets, etc]. What do you see? How do you feel?

Look deep into the Universe. What do you sense? What do you see? How do you fit into the Universe? Can you comprehend infinity?

Use all your senses.

Your sight. What do you see?

Your smell. Do you smell the trees, the flowers? What do you smell?

Your hearing. Do you hear the insects, the wind. What do you hear?

Your touch. Do things feel different at night? What do you feel?

Anything else? Do you sense anything else? What do you sense, and how?

Do you sense the wild creatures? Do you sense nature?

Chapter 19

Exercises to Get You Started

Connect to Mother Earth and Father Sky

This is a visualization exercise to get you grounded and focused. When you have become good at this exercise, you will be able to do it at any time when you feel that you are not focused on Mother Earth and Father Sky, or when you feel you are not connected to the animals.

Visualization is the art of mentally "seeing" something within your mind. The visualization concept can be used to help with, and prepare for, many situations in life. Athletes sometimes use visualization methods to prepare for various situations that might come up in a race, for example.

Before you begin this visualization exercise, it may help if you first go and look at a tree if you are able to do this.

Now, let's begin the exercise.

Stand where you have some space around you. You need space to outstretch your arms as you will become a tree and your arms will become branches. If you are like me and work with crystals, you may wish to put your favourite crystal in front of your feet and visualize that your crystal is the centre of the earth.

You may wish to do this exercise in privacy.

When you are ready, with your crystal at your feet, outstretch your arms and visualize your body becoming a tree.

Breathe slowly and deeply. Take 3 deep breaths. Slowly . . . . and deeply.

As you are taking those deep breaths, visualize yourself becoming an old oak tree or another kind of tree that you know well. Your arms are the branches. Your body is the trunk.

Breathe slowly and deeply to inhale beauty, wisdom and confidence, and exhale negativity and all harmful thoughts.

Now, from your big toes, your little toes, and the heels of your feet, visualize feeder roots coming out and growing deep into Mother Earth until they come to the crystal at the centre of Mother Earth. Wrap your feeder roots around the crystal at the centre of the earth, and bring this connection with Mother Earth up through the feeder roots into your body and into your heart. Feel that connection with Mother Earth connecting with your heart. Visualize yourself connecting with all the animals, all the creatures, on and in Mother Earth, on the surface, in the trees, in the ground, in the oceans, the seas, the rivers, the lakes, everywhere.

Now, without moving your head, visualize a beautiful night sky. In that night sky there is a beautiful star with your name on it. Bring the white light from that star down into your head, into your throat and into your heart. Visualize yourself connecting to the sky and to the universe, being connected with all the birds and insects and other creatures which fly in the air and in the sky.

Then say:-

"I am connected to Mother Earth, and all the animals on and within Mother Earth: the ground, the rivers and lakes, the oceans and seas.

I am connected to Father Sky and all the birds and insects and other creatures that fly in the sky. I am balanced. I am focused."

Then relax, knowing that you are connected to Mother Earth and to Father Sky, and to all the animals in the ground, on the ground, in the oceans, in the seas, rivers and lakes, in the air and in the sky.

You can do this exercise if you are tired or not getting a good animal communication, or just when you have had a busy day. It will help you relax and get centered and focused.

Now we are going to start.

When we set up our computers, we put in an antivirus programme. For animal communication or any energy work we do, we will surround ourselves in a white light or put ourselves in a white bubble. Visualize yourself surrounded by white light or inside a white bubble.

When we surf the net we sometimes get trojans or other viruses, and that is why we protect ourselves with computer antivirus programmes. When we communicate with animals we do not usually pick up any negative vibrations; but occasionally we may get these, and the white light or bubble protects us from negative energy so that we get positive communication with the animals.

Now we are going to grow our animal tail, and yes we do have an animal tail. Our residual "tail" is the coccyx at the base of the spine, inherited from our animal ancestors, but now very short and not visible externally in humans. The tail which we visualize will be our "telephone link" to the Animal Kingdom. It connects us with the heart of the Animal Kingdom and brings the Animal Kingdom to us. When we start animal communication, we use a tail as our connection. Later, as we gain experience, we can learn to go "wireless."

You can visualize any animal tail. Visualize this going down to the centre of the earth, to the crystal at the center of the earth.

Now connect to the heart of the Animal Kingdom at the centre of the earth, bring the heart of the Animal Kingdom up this tail into your heart, and connect your heart to the heart of the Animal Kingdom. Feel yourself connected with all the brothers and sisters in the Animal Kingdom.

Now, with a photograph or your pet nearby, you are ready to form your main connection. Focus on the picture, visualize that the animal is next to you, and connect to the animal.

If the animal is in the room, you can connect to him/her by looking at him/her, but do not stare at the animal or at his/her eyes as this may seem aggressive to the animal. On the other hand, if you are using a photograph, it is best to have the animal's eyes [in the photograph] in your vision.

If the animal is your pet, you will know the animal's history. If not your pet, then it helps if you can find out about the animal's history.

You can do the communication while you are sitting or standing.

Communicating.

Now fill your heart with love, and send that feeling of love to the animal's heart.

When you feel it is connected, you will say in your mind three times:

"The love in my heart overflows to your heart. We are connected."
"The love in my heart overflows to your heart. We are connected."
"The love in my heart overflows to your heart. We are connected."

Then you are ready to talk to your animal. You can start with any of the questions, if relevant, which we have listed for you in chapter 24 if you cannot at first think of anything to ask. Before you start, sometimes it is good to write down your questions in case you forget.

You can send communications as words, pictures, videos, sentences, feelings, smells; and the animal may send words, pictures, videos, sentences, feelings, smells, etc, back to you. Communicate with an open mind. It may be very fast and you will have to "grab" the information very quickly to assimilate it. Sometimes you might have to interpret what an animal is telling you, as their perspective of the world is from a different viewpoint.

Now let us do a recap

Relax and get ready to begin your animal communication.

If using a photo, have the photo ready.

If your pet is in the room, sit down with your pet.

Now put on your white light or white bubble, grow down your animal tail, and do your heart to heart connection with the animal.

When you feel that the connection is set up, begin communicating with your animal by giving him/her words, pictures, videos, sentences, feelings, smells; and receive the answers that he/she sends you. The answers may come very quickly, or gradually, or the animal may take time before responding, so wait for the replies if waiting is necessary.

Use your log sheet to keep a record on how you received the answers, so as to give you an idea as to the ways in which you as an individual can best communicate with animals. A sample log sheet can be found near the end of this book. Some people are more visual and get more pictures, some get more feelings, and some get words, sentences, videos, etc. We can think of it as something like a Skype session with your very best friend.

This will take some time, and lots of practice is all important to progressively improve and hone your animal communication skills.

If an animal does not want to talk to you, you should respect his/her wishes, but usually our companion animals love to talk to us once they realize that we are connected telepathically.

Always remember to ask your companion animal if there is something he/she wants to tell you. Do not get upset if it is something you do not like, because your animal has his/her own way of thinking. Perhaps you thought his/her favorite food was one thing but perhaps something you gave him as a treat a few months ago is something he likes more.

Pointers

The more you practise, the easier it becomes. Remember, at the beginning you may have some difficulty, but continue to practise.

This is not something which can be measured like a mathematics examination, as it has to be done from the heart.

What makes a good animal communicator is someone who keeps on talking to the animals and connecting to their hearts, and who can understand, assimilate and interpret what the animals are telling you.

Remember always to end by sending love to the animal and thanking him/her for talking to you.

Ask the animals questions in your own language as telepathy is a universal translator, and do not worry about language.

Communicating with a Horse

Chatty bird

CHAPTER 20

Visualization Exercise

This is a visualization exercise. For this exercise, you should have a photograph of your animal. After we have finished the exercise I will tell you how it has been used and how it has worked in two different situations.

I want you to look at the picture of your animal. When you think you have everything about that picture in your mind, I want you to close your eyes and visualize that picture in your mind. After you have done that, open your eyes, look at the picture and see if you have missed anything. Then look up if you have finished.

Let me tell you how you can use this exercise. We once had a lady in the classroom called Miss Noisy. She went home and came back the next day. On her way into the classroom her friend phoned her to say that she had lost her cat. By the way, this happened before technology routinely had pictures on mobile phones. Therefore we couldn't send the cat's picture through the phone. So we asked Miss Noisy: did she know the cat? She said: "Yes, and I also know where the cat first got lost. That's where they used to take the cat to sunbathe." So Miss Noisy visualized the cat, using animal communication skills and a heart to heart connection. Then she visualized the place that cat had to go back to, and asked the cat to return. The cat did go back, but Miss Noisy had too many noisy friends there that made the

Rosina Maria Arquati: The Life Journey of an Animal Communicator

cat run away. So we told Miss Noisy to do the same exercise the next day with just two people, being very quiet. That worked and the cat came back.

Another way of using this visualization exercise is for re-homing animals. I will give you examples after I tell you how to do it.

First, you sit down and do your communication with the animal. But before you even start, you have to think in your mind who is the right person to re-home that animal.

For instance, if you know that the animal doesn't like children, you have to visualize a family that doesn't have any children. Also, if the animal doesn't like men, you may have to think of a lady on her own. You have to visualize the right kind of human for that animal that would love and care for that animal for all his/her life. If it is a puppy or kitten, that can be fifteen years or longer. In that time span those owners have to support that animal, physically, emotionally and financially. It is unfair to an animal to go to a family which, as soon as the pet is sick, doesn't want to pay the veterinary bills because they are expensive.

You have to visualize the right human guardian for that particular animal. When you have achieved that, you proceed with your animal communication, and you send them that picture of the right human(s) which you have worked out are suitable for the animal. If the animal rejects them, looks unhappy, doesn't want to know, it could be that the animal isn't ready to be re-homed, he/she is still healing from being abandoned, and at that stage you stop the animal communication. If you do animal healing you can send healing to the animal.

When you send that picture to the animal and the animal looks happy, ask the animal to visualize himself with that family. Does the animal give you a positive feedback? Then, the final step: you visualize that animal being taken out of the animal shelter and going home with that perfect family for him/her.

I was working with some kittens at a shelter in Malaysia, a very busy shelter. I was working outside with some kittens as there was no air conditioning there. A man came in crying, with a ginger cat. He said that he had to give his cat up because his wife was pregnant and the whole family had made him give the cat up. He was very upset, he was actually crying. He also told us that the cat liked men more than women. The cat was left on the table while I was working. When I finished working with the kittens, I went to work with the ginger cat, giving healing, and communicating with him that we were going to help him to find a home by visualizing a home with a man who was coming to get him, and being happy. I told the cat to give a positive feedback for this home and he did. Then I visualized the cat going home. This was a beautiful cat but very stressed. He didn't like the environment he was in, because he was a well-loved pet. By the time I finished he was much calmer. Then suddenly I was called to go work in another area with a poodle. By the time I came back from working with the dog, the cat had gone. I got very worried because this area was vast and I had no idea what had happened to him and where he was, and I hoped he had not been put in this particular area as he was very stressed. When I enquired about him, I was told that two gay men came in looking for a cat and they fell in love with the ginger cat and took him home.

When I was in Singapore I worked with a group called Zeus, a very progressive type of animal shelter where they use animal communication and energy healing as they are my students. While there I always work with them. One day, they had two rescued puppy mill dogs left: two golden retrievers, called Jack and Jill. Jack had a promise of a home as he was healthy. But Jill was very sick as she had been kept in the puppy mill for intensive breeding until she was rescued; she was at risk of dying. The home that needed to take her in was in need of resources to pay for the large veterinary bills as she was on medication.

I worked with Jack and told him he was going to a nice home and he would be fine. I was asked if I could do anything for Jill. I told her that she was going to be looked after no matter how sick she would be, and she would be in the perfect home with landed property, a garden. She liked the idea of the garden and I "saw" her going home. Just when we were going out of the shelter someone phoned up to say they could afford the vet bills and could take her in. Jill was re-homed, alive, and living in landed property with other dogs, and returned to good health.

These are examples of using the visualization technique for re-homing and for lost animals. Does it work? Yes, it does work.

Rosina Communicating with Animals in theirHome

CHAPTER 21

Animals that have passed away

Yes, we can communicate with animals that have passed away. This is something that each individual has to work out on their own belief systems. What I am going to share with you now, is from my belief system: this comes from a fusion of my upbringing as a Catholic, my connection now with Buddhism and the Symbol of Mercy Guan Yin [Kwun Yam, Kwan Yin], and my New Age spiritual work. I believe that we occupy the body we are in now for a life time journey. When we die, our soul, our spirit, our light body whatever you want to call it, goes up on a journey.

I have respect for all the great religions, which teach us to be better people, to be compassionate and caring, to be kind. If we are Christians we might believe in Heaven. If we are Buddhists we might believe in Nirvana. For me, I use the concept of a kind of parallel universe and that's where our light body stays. Because we have been told so, and due to our religious beliefs, we see Heaven with Angels or Nirvana with Buddha. I see a place where there is a light being that can travel back and forth without any hurt or damage when they come to visit us on this world. When I see animals or people in the spirit world, I see happy healthy beings because that is what the spirit world is like. When we are due to reincarnate, just a piece of our spirit, our soul, our light body, comes back to reincarnate and starts a new journey into our new "rented accommodation" which is our physical body, and then a whole new life continues. But the original light body or essence is still in the spirit world, and this is what we can all connect to when we want to connect with our dear beloved animal friends.

When should we talk to an animal that has passed over into the spirit world? Time is needed to settle in on the other side and I believe the earliest it should be is normally two weeks after the animal has died. It gives the animal time to pass over into the spirit world, and gives humans time to grieve, mourn, and prepare the funeral. Here again, some people, if they are Buddhists, believe in 40 days or 47 days; you must go with your religious belief system.

On a very few occasions, when I have had some humans totally distressed about the loss of their beloved animal, I have conducted an animal communication three or four days after the animal has died. But that is in emergency "stressed-out" situations. When a person loses their pet, their loved one, their child, their husband, their confidant, or their best friend, the person may become highly stressed and emotionally disturbed. And grief, for some people who lose a pet, can be even greater than when losing a human loved one.

Scamp

I believe that there are animals that have close connections with us, who never leave us. They are always with us, and come back when they need us and when we need them. I have been explaining this for years in workshops and one day it actually happened to me.

My husband had finished a work contract, and didn't know what he was going to do next. When he was a young boy, he had a tricolor border collie called Scamp. I had never physically met Scamp as Scamp had died before I first met my husband-to-be. I had met and known his other dogs, Socrates and Zack.

At this time, we had to move house. As we were clearing out the house and moving things around, I suddenly saw a tricolor border collie walking beside my husband. What you have to understand is that this is a very normal occurrence for me, so I wasn't frightened. I didn't say anything at first because I assumed it was Scamp. When I told my husband later that I had seen Scamp, my husband replied "Are you sure that it was Scamp?" I felt a bit dumb at first, but I knew that if I saw the dog again I would check that it was him.

Then again I saw my husband and the dog walking across the room as we were moving things in the room. Then I saw him again in the corridor. This time I was prepared, and I asked the dog "Are you Scamp?" The dog replied "Yes." Then I asked him "What are you doing here after all these years?" The dog simply said "My human needs me."

After that my husband was offered a job overseas, where there were lots of border collies, and Scamp was back in my husband's heart once more.

Big Dog and Little Dog

There was another instance when I went to see a dying dog. For some reason I felt that the dog was big. But, I have learned never to assume anything. When I rang the doorbell, the maid opened the door, and there I saw by the corridor a big German Shepherd who then ran off into a room. Then the lady owner came out holding a very small dog. By then I was confused, as I could have sworn that I had seen a German Shepherd dog.

The lady came and sat next to me holding a beautiful but very sick dog. Then, while talking to her, I mentioned "I thought you had a big German Shepherd." She said "No." Then I told her what I had seen. "How strange," she said, "a few weeks ago, the owner of the house came in and said that he had felt the presence of his old dead dog, a German Shepherd."

The German Shepherd dog was waiting for the little dog to pass on, when he would take him into the spirit world. This particular animal was a wonderful pet, kind and loving, and knew that the little sick dog needed help.

Mr Rabbit

I was in an animal communication session for a rabbit which had passed away, a very lovely rabbit who had passed over. I saw him as living in a beautiful garden with beautiful plants. The rabbit showed me that he was very happy, active, running around, and sent love to his human. Then the rabbit asked me to thank his human for the pay rise! I was a little confused, and I asked the [human] client, "Have you had a pay rise?" She said, "Yes."

Then Mr Rabbit said, "Thank you for all the extra things you bought for me with the money," and I passed this message on to the human guardian, who then began to cry. She told me that she had bought some new things and some better hay for Mr Rabbit, and had made his home more beautiful. Mr Rabbit loved his human, and was happy now in his spirit life. He had asked for very little, and had been happy with the life he had had with his human.

When souls, "light-beings", are received into the spirit world they can become happy and healthy in the spiritual senses of the words. There is nothing to fear about the spirit world. I tell my students we should have more fear of the living humans. The living can do much more harm than the dead, and as you work more and more with animals that have passed over you will understand what I am trying to convey.

Communicating with Cats

Do animals lie?

Animals do have feelings and emotions just like us, and if they do, they can also lie.

My son Smoky Quartz: Oh dear! a little troublesome one, the only dog I ever rescued as a puppy. I had no prior experience of looking after puppies. Smoky was a very sick two month old abandoned Pomeranian puppy that was to be fostered. The shelter could not look after him. Could I take him in? I had an in-house vet, and I was an energy healer, so it would be the right place for a very sick puppy to go. We took him in and for two weeks I did nothing but nurse this poor sickly puppy.

Then it was time for prospective adopters to come and look at the puppy, so that he could be re-homed. As I said, I very seldom took puppies in, I usually took older dogs, sometimes sick ones, because they were much harder for the shelters to re-home. We had the facilities to look after them and we had somewhere safe for them to die. Our home was like a hospice and a young puppy wasn't something that would usually fit in.

When the people came to inspect the puppy, he was still in isolation because he had a very bad skin problem. When people wanted a lively dog he would play dead; when they wanted a quiet dog he would not stop barking; when they wanted a healthy dog he would pull his hair up, which wasn't very much hair at that time, and would show his scabs. It was soon clear that this dog didn't want to leave our house and I had to make a decision whether or not I should keep him. I announced this to my husband, and when I told him he was in shock. It was like a woman telling her husband that after menopause she was having a baby. My husband started pacing up and down. I asked him what was wrong. He said: "Do you realize that by the time the puppy is 15 years old, you will be a "senior citizen"? "Yes," I said, "I thought of that too, so I'll make sure he is well covered in my will; I intend to live to a ripe old age." Most of the women in my family do live long, usually they live on till they are 90, and my auntie is now 100.

But what did I know about puppies? I had only ever rescued old dogs. So I went to my two female dogs and asked them if we should keep this puppy and would they help me. The two girls said, "No way, this is a problem kid." So I took my woes to my two boy dogs Jasper and Topaz. Topaz was a real He-Man; Jasper on the other hand had a very feminine touch. Obviously the two boys were not as experienced with puppies as the girls, and they said yes. Jasper and Topaz didn't like each other very much but they said they would help me in bringing up the puppy.

During one of my classes one of the students forgot to bring a photo of her animal and knowing that Smoky was a very talkative dog I gave her a photo of Smoky Quartz and said to her: "Ask him if he likes Jasper and Topaz." His reply was as follows: "Jasper bullies me and Topaz bites me." When the student gave me this information I burst into tears laughing, this sounded just like my son. In fact he, Smokey Quartz, had bitten Topaz and had bullied Jasper.

So animals do sometimes lie, just like the ginger cat I mention in the next chapter who said that it was the black cat that terrorized him.

As a matter of interest, Smoky has grown up to be a fine young man. Topaz and Jasper are now in the spirit world, and they are still looking after him.

Communicating with fishes

CHAPTER 23

Sharing some Animal Communication Experiences With You

What's in a name?

Giving your animals good names is important. It gives the animals positive energies and vibrations. My dogs are now all given names of crystals. These doggies were abandoned, and they all came from rescue shelters. They had not been properly cared for, had been kept in poor conditions, they were sick when they came to us. With treatment, care and love, and being given positive names, they blossomed, and now they are known as The Aristocratic Pomeranians.

On one occasion during an animal communication session, a lady told me about the dog she took in. She had given the dog a standard old-fashioned Korean name, but the dog would never come to her when she called the name. One night they were both watching television, and Beyoncé was on. The lady said, "Beyoncé, she is so pretty," and the dog came and sat on the sofa with her. After that, when the lady said "Beyoncé", the dog would come to her. This dog chose her own name. As I communicated with the doggy, she told me that the old name did not suit her. The doggy knew that she was beautiful, and I had to agree with her.

The dog and the sports car

Working as a professional animal communicator over the years has been rewarding. Some of my case studies are very funny and very interesting. One interesting case study was a dog. The lady and I were doing a private consultation for the dog and suddenly the dog showed me a black sports car. The dog was sitting rather tightly at the back of this sports car but was enjoying the ride. I assumed from this that this was the owner's car.

The Dog and the Sports car

I said to the lady: "Your dog loves going in the sports car."

She said "We don't have a sports car, Rosina, but it is funny you should mention this. A few weeks ago, my husband suggested we buy a sports car and I told him it was too expensive."

"Oh," I said."

Then we continued talking, and during that time her husband came in and we shared the story of the sports car.

The husband smiled, looked at me and then at his wife. "Well," he said, "the dog and I decided on the color of the spots car we are going to get, and I paid a deposit on it."

The man, instead of sharing the information about the car he wanted to buy with his wife, had shared the information with the dog. He and the dog had made a decision on which sports car they were going to buy and to this day I don't know if the dog told the human to tell me or if the dog decided just to tell me to make sure he got his sports car.

The dog and the cookie monster

I worked with an old and very sick dog for a long time. He was not only sick but almost blind. I knew the home where the dog lived.

One night I was called to the veterinary hospital as the dog had been taken seriously ill and the human guardian wanted to know if he missed the other dogs. I asked the dog if he missed the other dogs. Suddenly the dog showed me a blue ball-like object. I knew the owners very well, and blue was not part of their colour scheme. I told the husband, and he said he would phone the maid to check the front room. The maid did so, and opposite to where the dog had been sitting was a rather round blue cookie monster. The dog had been staring at this cookie monster since Christmas, and it was now March, and this cookie monster had become his best friend. The dog, with very little eyesight, hadn't realized it wasn't another dog. He thought of it as his best friend who couldn't run around like he could and so just sat on the chair opposite. The owner brought in the cookie monster for the dog, and they got along well together.

The black cat and the ginger cat

When I went to see these cats, I was told that the black cat was attacking the ginger cat. The ginger cat was very sweet and came up to me and told me that the black cat was hitting him. He said that he had never done anything wrong, and I said "OK, you poor thing." He really sucked me in, I felt so sorry for him. And I thought for a moment, this sounds like my own dog Smokey; he said he never did anything wrong but he was the one that caused the entire problem. I said to the ginger cat: "Just wait a moment, I want to talk to the black cat." I talked to the black cat and he told me that the ginger cat was terrorizing him. He would run behind him and scratch him. Of course he would fight back. I conveyed this message to the owners. And they said they thought this might be happening. They set up a monitor, and, lo and behold, it was the ginger cat that was starting the fights.

Cat scared of neighbor's dog

Another case study was a cat that suddenly started weeing on the carpet. In Hong Kong where we live, the flats are really small. This flat was about 500 square feet, and the front door opened up directly to the front room, where the cat would sit during the day.

When I talked to the cat she told me that the dog was going to come through the door and eat her. Now, the guardian didn't have a dog. The flat was right next door to the lift. I asked if any of the neighbors had a dog. She said the lady in the corner flat had just got a puppy. What had been happening was that the puppy was sniffing at the door while waiting for the lift and the cat became frightened that the pup was going to come through the door and attack her.

I talked to the guardian and asked if she was willing to talk to the neighbor at the end of the corridor and ask her to walk the dog on the other side, lift him up, and not let him sniff at the door. She said the neighbor was very friendly and she would do this. I went back into communication with the cat and assured her that she was safe in the front room; the dog couldn't get through the door no matter what happened. But her mummy would talk to the neighbor and make sure the dog wouldn't sniff at the door.

We put everything into action and the cat stopped weeing on the carpet.

St. Bernard dog

Animal communications come in various ways. I was once doing a communication with a St. Bernard dog, and he fell asleep behind me.

As often happens, the guardian said: "One more question Rosina for our dog. Could you ask him what he likes to eat." This was a very long time ago, with a Chinese family. The dog gave me a Garfield bubble. I had never received a bubble before. Inside the bubble image was a thick juicy steak. I have lived in Hong Kong for a very long time, and at BBQs here the steaks are usually quite thin, and steaks being cooked in other ways are usually thin too.

From the cartoon bubble image I received, I realized that the dog liked to dream and I passed this on very carefully and simply to the humans: "Your dog loves to dream."

They said "Yes, he does."

I was hesitant. Then I said: "Your dog likes thick, juicy, medium rare steaks."

The human replied: "Yes, we have a small balcony and sometimes we have BBQs. We order the meat from the only butcher in this town that has Australian steaks and we give the dog Aussie steaks."

When I left I heard the dog say: "Hmm, juicy steaks tonight," and heard the clients phoning in the order.

Fried rice

Another time, when I was conducting an animal communication, the guardian asked who he liked best, because he lived between her and the mother. The dog said that he liked the mother. As I continued with the communication, I could smell fried rice. No one was cooking, so I passed this on to the owner: "Your dog likes fried rice." She was very insistent that her dog only ate dog food, and she never gave him fried rice. I said "OK." Again the smell of fried rice came in during the animal communication, and I told the owner that the dog would like to eat fried rice. She said he couldn't have it. Just before I left, I got the smell of fried rice yet again. I told the lady, "I don't know why, but your dog likes fried rice." Three weeks later she emailed me to tell me that her mother had owned up that she fed the dog fried rice.

Financial times

Another case study. The human guardian asked me what was the dog's favorite time? The dog said: "The money time." The guardian and I looked at each other. What did that mean? The maid came out of the kitchen and reminded the owner that the only times that the family ever sat down together were the morning and evening to watch the financial report. The dog didn't just like the money time, he liked the time the whole family sat down to watch the financial report and the dog would sit down with them.

The bag dog

In another case study when I was communicating with a large size cocker spaniel, whose guardian was a very small Chinese lady, the dog was showing me a big Louis Vuitton bag. I kept on looking at the dog and wondered what he really wanted to tell me. I asked the guardian: "Do people in this house like bags?" She said yes, her mother did. But the dog continued to show me big bags and he himself sitting in one. I was very confused, because the human guardian was very small and the dog was quite big. It would be almost impossible for her to carry the dog in the bag as he wasn't a bag size dog. So I said to the guardian, "I feel that your dog likes being carried in a bag, if he could fit into one," to which she replied "Every time we take him out, we take him out in a bag even though he is a big dog!"

Burberry material

Again, during an animal communication for a dog, an oblong strip of Burberry material appeared. "Hmm," I thought, "a Hong Kong dog." I told the owner that the dog liked Burberry material but I couldn't understand why? It was a small piece that I saw. The lady said: "Wait a moment." She got up, went into the kitchen and came back with a head band which people put on cocker spaniels so that their ears don't get in the food. The headband was made of Burberry material. The dog didn't like the material but when he saw the head band, which was Burberry, it meant it was food time and he enjoyed eating.

The toy

Another time I was doing an animal communication and this time information came in like a video. The guardians had asked me, "What is the dog's favorite toy?" I suddenly felt myself becoming the eyes of the dog, going into the kitchen and looking up into the cupboard. In the cupboard was a shape. It wasn't quite straightforward, but it looked like a ball. I told the owners that the dog's ball which was his favorite toy was in the kitchen cupboard. They said yes, it was broken, and they had put it in the kitchen cupboard.

The Party Animal

Another time, another case study. I was sent out to see a dog. I was told this dog was naughty. When I got there it was a beautiful golden retriever who sat next to me with a beautiful bandana around his neck. He was about 4 years old and the humans treated him as their son. I looked at the dog and looked at the human guardians. Wow, if this was a naughty dog his guardians didn't know how lucky they were.

So I asked the owners what was the problem. They said when they had BBQs and parties on their patio, the dog started stealing food from the table, taking food out of people's hands, and would jump around. They were concerned because normally they would have children at these events.

I sat down and started to communicate to the dog what the humans had told me. He very simply said: "But I am only enjoying the party and doing what they are doing." I then sat back and looked at it from the dog's point of view. Yes, he was right: at BBQs people take food off the tables, people take food out of people's hands, and, of course, after a few glasses of wine people get lively and start dancing.

We negotiated with the dog that every time it was a BBQ or a party, he would have a special plate just for him and that would be his party plate. So he wouldn't need to go to the table to get food from people because he would have his own special party plate served in a very special place, and he could enjoy the social event.

The pigeon

Together with one of my students, I was walking to the New Age Shop in Hong Kong to take the morning meditation, but decided to go through the alley way into the shop. I was busy talking when my student suddenly noticed a pigeon struggling on the ground as it couldn't fly. We didn't know what to do. My first reaction was to talk to the bird, but first we wanted to see if the shop had a box in which to keep the bird if we could catch it. I asked the pigeon to stay there and try not to move too far, even though it was frightened.

We went into the shop and found a suitable box and also checked whether they would take the bird in if we caught it, as that particular night I was leaving for London to visit my mother. The student was also calling the SPCA to see what we could do for the pigeon. I asked a staff member in the shop to come with me because the pigeon was trying to escape.

When we went back to the alley way the pigeon was still there. I asked the staff to stay quiet so I could have time to talk to the pigeon. The pigeon's first reaction was to run from me, but I said: "Don't do that, we are trying to help you". The pigeon suddenly stopped, and I sat down and told the pigeon that we needed to get some medical help as we were unable to help at this stage. I had a very lightweight towel in my hand, of very thin cotton material. I laid it over the pigeon, which was actually in the gutter. It didn't try to move. It looked into my eyes, and once again I sat down to explain what I was going to do. I put the towel over its back so I wouldn't hurt the wing when I picked it up. I wanted it to understand that we didn't want to hurt it. We wanted to bring it to a good home where someone could look after it. The pigeon looked at me and said: "It is ok to pick me up." Then I went behind it, picked it up very gently and put it inside the box. It didn't flutter, it wasn't frightened anymore.

We took the pigeon back into the New Age Shop where other staff members gave it some Bach flower remedy and nursed it until one of the staff could take it home that evening. Connecting to the bird telepathically helped to save it. I, on the other hand, had to fly out to the UK to visit my 93 year old mother.

Bubo

The lost dog in Singapore. I was working in Singapore as an animal communicator one night, together with a Singapore lady named Lynda. Lynda and I went out to dinner by the beach. We had a nice evening and on our way to the car we noticed a little Schnauzer running around. He looked lost and was very busy sniffing. We didn't want to pick him up as we hoped that he would know his way home. But we decided to follow this little dog as he sniffed and rushed around. I asked him for his name as he was sniffing the trees. He said he was too busy he didn't have time to talk to me, he was enjoying himself.

We followed him for about 25 minutes, until he turned down a side street. He stopped and I managed to ask him where he lived. He said: "In a house with a big light, a car and a big gate." I looked around for the nearest place and knocked on the door. It was the only one with the lights on. There was another dog there and he barked. The owner there said that the schnauzer that was running around was not his. By this time we were beginning to get worried because the little dog didn't seem to know his way home. Then suddenly a car came up and the Schnauzer nearly got hit. This is the time when Lynda and I decided to take action and went to catch the little Schnauzer. We caught him and put him in the car. He sat very happily on my lap, as we started to drive off.

The houses in this area all looked very similar to what he described. It was coming up to midnight and I didn't want to knock on anybody else's door. So Lynda and I decided we would take the dog to stay with her. She would phone the SPCA and find information on the internet that night, and in the morning we would check in whether anybody was missing a dog.

On the way through the tunnel, he said: "You are going the wrong way, I don't want to go through the tunnel, I don't live this way."
"Yes," I said, "You don't live this way, but this is where you are going to stay tonight with Auntie Lynda, so calm down."

"No problem," he said, "this is an adventure."

He then turned around and told me: my lap was too skinny, my legs were not comfortable.

I asked him, "Is the person whose lap you usually sit on fatter than me?"

He said, "Much more comfortable, much more comfortable, and bigger."

So Lynda asked me to ask his name, and what came through was something like "Bubo, Bubo," but it was not clear.

Rosina Maria Arquati: The Life Journey of an Animal Communicator

We thought no more about it and we took the young man home and did as she said: put up notices, contacted the SPCA, the government department, and all the right bodies. In the morning when she came to pick me up she told me that Bubo's human guardian had been found and she had an accent. We were going to deliver Bubo back to his mummy.

We drove down the street to a location not far from where we had picked him up. We stopped at the house and yes, the house had a big gate, a car in the drive and a light at the side. The guardian was French and she was slim, and the son who was with her was also slim.

I said to the lady, "I am sorry but I have to ask: is there a fatter person in this house? I ask because the dog told me that my legs were not comfortable because they were too skinny."

She laughed and said her older son was rather tubby and Bubo would sit on his lap.

Then she went to call her dog, it sounded something like "Bubo, Bubo," but with a French accent. Lynda and I looked at each other and burst out laughing: the dog's name was right but it had a French accent. We were happy that we left Bubo at the house with his mummy and the son.

Chapter 24

Let's Chat

When talking with your pets, make it fun and easy to understand. Simple questions enable simple answers.

Very young puppies and kittens, under about five months of age, as well as very young animals generally, like to talk like babies, and so you may find some of the answers a little "gibberish" and difficult to understand.

As young animals grow, after five months or so for puppies and kittens, they become "toddlers", and continue to gain life experience, enabling them to answer your questions more clearly.

In this chapter, I offer some ideas for simple questions you can ask your pets for starters. If your pet does not answer, you may need to rephrase the question as the animal might not have understood it clearly. A good animal communicator is also a good "detective." Sometimes you may need to ask more than one question, two, three, occasionally more, to obtain an answer from the animal to a question asked by the animal's human guardian. Also consider the animal's nature and character when asking questions.

Remember, when asking animals questions, you can do it in different dimensions, not merely words and sentences. For example, to ask whether an animal is happy or sad, you can send the question in feelings of happy or sad, combined with the words "Are you happy or sad?"

To ask an animal what he/she likes to eat, you can show, when sending the question, different kinds of food to see which food(s) he/she favours. Remember to have fun when asking questions.

Communicate in ways which work best for the animal and for you. If you are better at visualization, send pictures, "videos", etc. If you communicate with feelings, then send feelings. If you like words, then you can try words.

Try also to think not only in words themselves, but also in concepts. Some people find this easy, some don't. In some human languages, a "word" may represent a concept, not just a narrow meaning: especially, in Chinese, a single character often represents a concept, and then characters are put together to create a more specific meaning.

Don't be constricted by one single approach. To be a good animal communicator, you need to be creative and be a "detective."

In nature, there are many dimensions of communication (see Chapter 27). Remember this when communicating with animals. In particular, when communicating with animals, have a friendly non-aggressive body posture. If speaking, speak in a calm friendly tone of voice. In general, do not stare at an animal as this may be perceived as aggressive. Also adopt, yourself, a positive happy state of mind so that you transmit positive friendly feelings and communication.

So have fun chatting with animals. Have fun playing with questions.

What shall we talk about?

If you are having difficulty thinking of anything to chat about, here are some example questions for starters.

Some examples of general questions for animals of many species:
Is the weather here too hot/cold?
Do you like the air conditioner/heater?
Are you happy with me?
Who do you like?
What do you like? What do you dislike?
Is there anything you need or want?
Do you like other animals?Which animals?
Is there anything you want to tell us or me?
What do you like to do?
What are your favorite places? Favorite toys? Favourite foods?
Do you like living in a flat / apartment?
Do you like the maid?
Is the maid kind to you?

Some example questions for dogs
Do you like swimming in the doggie pool?
Do you like to go out? Where? When?
Do you like other dogs?
Have you been to the beach?
Do you like going to kennels?
Do you like the maid?
Do you go for long walks / short walks?

Some example questions for cats:
Are you happy on your own?
Do you like your home?
How do you feel about dogs?
Do you like your cat box?
Would you like a companion cat?
Do you like other cats?

Some example questions for horses:
Is it too hot to race in hot summers?

Have you ever been mistreated?
Do you mind going into a trailer?
What do you eat?
Do you like racing?
Do you have a stall?
Are the staff kind to you?
Are the trainers kind to you?

Some example questions for expatriate animals:
Do you like it here?
Do you like the flat?
Is the flat big enough for you?
Is the pollution affecting you?
Are you missing your old home?
Is the humidity affecting you?
Do you miss the garden?
Do you miss your friends?
Do you like the maid (name)?
Do you like going to the kennels?
Is your maid kind to you?

Some example questions for rabbits and guinea pigs
Is your hay good?
Is your home clean?
Is your digestion good?
Do you get enough good water to drink?
Do you have enough space?
Are you comfortable?
Is it too hot or too cold?
Do you get enough exercise?
Are you happy here?
What do you need?
Do you get enough vitamin C? (Especially guinea pigs)

Do you get the idea?
For other species, consider the needs of that species and the ways in which they live, and chat about their lives, their needs, their feelings.

So how did you get along chatting with your animal friend(s)?

As with humans, some animals are extrovert and communicate easily and openly. Other animals are more introvert and so you need to warm up with them in gentle friendly chat before starting the questions.

When there are more than one animal, you can consider it like a cocktail party. Other animals may interrupt your chatting with one animal. You must be polite and explain to the others that you will talk with them soon.

Occasionally an animal asks me why it has taken so long for a human to communicate like this. "I've been trying to communicate with humans like this for years!" they tell me.

Be open and receptive to receive messages in any format. Perhaps you sent pictures but the response comes in "words"; or you sent words and the reply is in pictures.

Remember that each animal is an individual, and so each animal communication is different.

If you find yourself communicating with an animal and his/her human, be aware that animal communication cannot be carried out by proxy. The communication should be made with the individual animal and his/her real/actual owner/keeper/guardian. It is generally unwise to attempt animal communication with/through third-parties/friends/etc, because this easily cases confusion and misunderstanding.

Rosina and a wild blond hedgehog under treatment
and rehabilitation in a wildlife rescue centre

Energy healing and communication for a rescued stray mongrel dog

Ethics

Code of Conduct

ETHICS AND CONDUCT OF ANIMAL COMMUNICATORS:

1. The good animal communicator cares about animals and cares about people.
2. We work to facilitate understanding between humans and animals, and particularly to help the human guardians to understand their animals.
3. We strive to promote empathy, sympathy, and compassion towards animals.
4. We respect the guardians' privacy and confidentiality, and so we communicate with confidentiality.
5. We do not judge or condemn, but rather help people to progress in understanding animals.
6. We work to achieve positive progress, happiness and understanding.
7. We should not offer information that might make a person or animal feel worse.
8. We understand, and help others to understand, that animals can teach us as well as learn from us, that animals want to communicate with us and to develop mutual understanding with us, and that this can be achieved.

9. We want people to care about animals, and to understand that animals have feelings and emotions, and so we work to spread knowledge and appreciation of this concept and fact. In doing this, we hope to see an end to abandonment.

10. We understand that people live in different cultures, and we aim to educate and help, not criticize.

11. It is our aim to help and guide people to understand and value human-animal bonds and inter-relations, and also to understand that our stress and emotions carry over to animals.

12. We understand, and we strive to help others understand, that we are part of nature and of the world of living beings, and so we endeavor to spread the knowledge and commitment to respect animals and to respect the environment, understanding that we are all inter-connected.

13. We feel empathy and sympathy with animals.

14. Our intention is to help animals, and so to do no harm to animals. In our endeavors to do no harm, we try to embrace and practise the concepts of "No-kill" and "Cruelty-free" to the best of our individual abilities. ("No-kill" does not rule out true euthanasia when this is justified and necessary to end incurable suffering and/or advanced terminal illness.)

15. We take care so that we do not place ourselves or others into avoidable situations of real or potential danger.

16. We are motivated by compassion for all beings, and our desire to help.

17. We do not practise speciesism. We care about all life, including vertebrates and invertebrates, and we care too about nature.

18. Animal communicators who are not veterinarians willingly refer animals to veterinarians for veterinary diagnosis and treatment.

19. We are happy to co-operate, liaise, and work with those veterinarians who are open to this.

20. When communicating with an animal, our practice is to communicate with the individual animal and with his/her actual/

real owner/keeper/guardian if a human is involved. We do not communicate through third-parties/friends/etc because this can cause confusion and misunderstanding. Animal communication cannot be carried out by proxy.

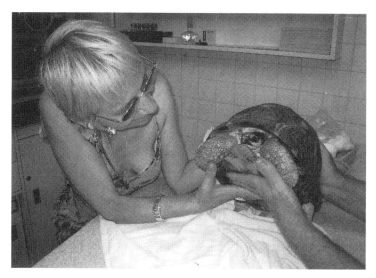

Communicating with a tortoise in a veterinary clinic

Q&A: Questions & Answers

1. **What is Animal Communication?**

   Animal Communication is a method of communicating with animals telepathically.

2. **Do all animals have telepathic abilities?**

   Yes, all animals have telepathic abilities.

3. **Do humans have telepathic abilities?**

   Yes, most humans have telepathic abilities, but only a small percentage of people can tap into it naturally.

4. **How does an animal feel when it is communicating with an animal communicator?**

   The animal does not feel anything, regardless of whether it is awake or asleep during communication.

5. My dog is afraid of strangers—will there be any problems trying to communicate with it?

To initiate a communication session, animal communicators will introduce themselves and tell the animal their intentions of communication. For assurance, the animal will also be informed that it has got its human guardian's permission to communicate. Most of the time, the animal will be willing to communicate if it knows that the communication session is for its own good.

6. Will animals always tell the truth?

Not always. Animals are like humans; some are honest and some are not. Animals might lie to protect themselves and their humans, but sometimes they do it out of sheer mischief.

7. Can animal communication correct undesirable behaviors in animals?

Animal communication can help you understand why the animals exhibit certain undesirable behaviors but most of the time, merely communicating with them cannot bring about significant changes. The owners must first play an active role in rectifying the animals' behaviors. If the desired behaviors are not exhibited even after the owner's corrections, the help of an animal trainer might have to be introduced.

8. Can telepathic animal communication hurt the animals?

Telepathic communication is natural to animals and does not harm them. Animal communication is for good, for kindness, for compassion: it should never be abused to exploit or harm people, animals or nature.

9. Can one communicate with deceased animals?

Yes, but communication with a deceased animal is best done after it has departed for about 2-3 weeks. If the human guardian has a dire need to communicate with a recently deceased animal, an allowance of at least 3 days should be made before initiating communication.

10. Does the animal have to be present physically in order to conduct an animal communication session?

No. An animal communicator will only need a recent photograph of the animal, together with some details such as the animals' breed, sex and age to conduct animal communication.

11. Do our pets have emotions?

Just like us, all animals have souls, emotions and thoughts.

12. How does an animal communicator get information from the animals?

Each animal communicator receives information in different ways. The most common ways are in forms such as images, 'words', sensations, feelings, intuition and concepts. Some animal communicators also use automatic writing and automatic drawing to get information from the animals.

13. Why do people want to communicate with animals?

The list of reasons why people want to communicate with animals is never-ending. There are many reasons why people wish to communicate with animals and the reasons vary according to each individual and their needs. A few of such reasons include helping the animal cope with changes in its environment (moving house, a new family member, the owner leaving for a trip, etc); to find out his/her likes and dislikes; or if he/she has any physical problems such as pains or aches. However, it is important to note that animal communication can never be a substitute for professional veterinary care.

14. Is it true that animal communication can be used to connect/talk to all animals, including wildlife and domestic animals?

Yes. Animal communication can be used to connect/talk to all animals, including wildlife and domesticated ones.

15. Are men or women better at animal communication?

There are fewer men who attend the animal communication workshops, but those who do complete the workshop sessions turn out to be quite good animal communicators. Anyone can pick up animal communication, if they are focused and have sufficient practice and interest.

16. Is practice needed for animal communication?

Practice is essential once you start learning animal communication, in order to improve yourself.

17. Why do you use the term "guardian".

As we come to understand and empathize with animals, we come to appreciate that animals are not chattels to own and dispose of at will. The animals share our lives with us just as human family members do. Our role is to care for and nurture animals, and so we often avoid calling ourselves the "owners" of animals. Instead, we often use terms like "guardian" or similar terms. This book uses terms such as "human", "guardian", and "human guardian"

18 ... What should I do if my animal is sick?

You should seek prompt professional veterinary advice and care. Usually this will involve having the animal promptly examined by a veterinarian for diagnosis, treatment and follow up care. Also, you can prevent many diseases and injuries by proper care and preventive programmes, which include veterinary advice and procedures, and may include veterinary vaccinations to prevent serious infectious diseases, healthy food/diet, parasite prevention, dental care and body care, proper grooming, proper weight management, and other measures to benefit the animal both physically and psychologically. Animal communication can help with mutual understanding and communication between you and the animal. Animal communication is complementary to veterinary care, but is never a substitute or alternative to it. Professional veterinary care is very important for animals.

Dimensions of Communication

This book chiefly focuses on the telepathic aspects of communicating with animals, mainly because this is a universal way to communicate between all species.

Many of us since childhood have been indoctrinated to believe that we are some kind of "superior beings" or "superior species". Usually we are told that we are the most intelligent species, and therefore superior. This idea is largely based on defining "intelligence" as human intelligence. But if we were to define "intelligence" with the inclusion of a successful ability to live in harmony with Nature and the Environment, then we humans might rate pretty low on the intelligence scale! Isn't protection of one's life support Mother Nature what an intelligent being would do? In the vast Universe in which we are a tiny part, can we sensibly define intelligence based on just one species?

So we need to put aside preconceptions and human vanity, and move forward with open minds.

Human scientists are only just beginning to appreciate that many species have languages and complex communication forms, yet we humans still do not understand them: whale songs, bird songs in different dialects, the real meanings of different forms of vocalizations from dogs and cats, and so on seemingly *ad infinitum*.

Some teachers, who teach humans how to communicate more effectively with other humans, tell us that up to 70% of human-to-human communication is by body language, not words. You know that when you meet another person, you receive messages and feelings from their body language before any spoken word is uttered.

━━━━━━━━━

It would take many books to attempt to explain the multitudinous ways in which different species communicate, and that is outside the scope of this book right now. In these complex studies, we humans are still beginners. Telepathy can be the universal translator.

Nevertheless, if we wish to understand animals and communicate with animals, it is good for us to be aware of the many ways in which communications are carried out, not only in humans, but also in many species.

By spending time with animals, we can begin to understand the ways of communication of those animals with which we share our lives, even though it may be just the beginning of our comprehension.

The following section lists out some ways in which animals, whether human or non-human, are believed to communicate.

The list is not exhaustive.

━━━━━━━━━

1. *Telepathy*

2. *Vocalizations and Making Sounds*

    a. "Words", such as humans often use
    b. Sounds with meanings: special vocalizations of prairie dogs, a purring cat, a growling dog, a screaming human
    c. Whale songs
    d. Bird songs and dialects
    e. Insect sounds such as those of cicada tymbals
    f. Sounds from Nature such as thunder
    g. Other ways of communicating using sounds

3. *Auditory [Hearing Sounds]*
A way to receive communications which have been sent as sounds: hearing a dog bark, receiving words spoken by another human, enjoying bird songs in Nature, animals hearing mating calls from other animals, and more.

4. *Visual*

    a. Human dancing
    b. Bird dances, eg courtship, wooing
    c. Pointing
    d. Gazing
    e. Sign language, eg communications by deaf people, rude gestures
    f. Facial expressions, postures, looking away [non-aggression]
    e. Body language: an aggressive human, a submissive dog, an annoyed cat, a frightened rabbit
    f. Movements and behaviors: a female cat on heat, a dog [or human] looking away [non-aggression]
    g. Reading and writing

5. **Physical actions:** running away, turning one's back

6. **Olfactory [Smell, Scents, Odours]**

   a. Conscious: perfumes, female dog in heat, body odours
   b. Subconscious: pheromones

7. **Electrical:** certain aquatic/marine creatures have sensors to detect electrical impulses from other creatures

8. **Vibrations**

9. **Intuitive**

10. **Other:** As you spend time practising communicating with animals, you may notice even more ways in which animals communicate

CHAPTER 28

Energy Healing

Many people ask me about Energy Healing for animals.

It is important to remember that this is complementary to other therapies, not a substitute.

Professional veterinary care by a registered veterinarian is always important.

Outline of Energy Healing Concepts

Although Energy Healing might not strictly be a part of Animal Communication, some animal communicators do train in this modality and may use it in their work to help animals with which they communicate. The concept is therefore briefly outlined in this chapter.

Energy Healing is a non-invasive treatment modality using energy fields channeled by the practitioner. The energy comes from the Universe. Energy is abundant in the Universe.

The practitioner may carry out the treatment through laying on hands or keeping them close to the animal, or by distant healing, so that the energy then starts to flow into the animal to address the *dis-ease* and the *emotions* of the animal.

Einstein discovered that: energy (e) = mass (m) x the square of a constant (c), giving us the famous equation e = mc^2 (The constant 'c' equals the speed of light, light itself being a form of energy.) This shows that energy and mass are related. An animal has both mass and energy.

Natural healing processes in the body of an animal use energy obtained from the Universe through food, water, air, and warmth.

Life itself needs and uses such energy. Energy Healing helps to channel energy and to enhance and balance the energy field of the animal.

What is Reiki for Animals?

Reiki is a complementary procedure which helps to calm an animal, and relax an animal when he/she is stressed or has emotional or physical problems or is ill. The natural intrinsic healing processes within an animal are better able to function in an animal which is more calm and relaxed and peaceful and less stressed. Reiki is complementary to treatment by a veterinarian. Reiki is **never** a substitute for professional veterinary care and treatment.

Reiki is a hands-on procedure, carried out in a relaxed and calm manner to help the animal feel calmer and less stressed.

Each animal is an individual. Usually the animal will lay there peacefully through the session, and is relaxed, happy and contented.

Animals can suffer from many ailments, some curable and some not, some mild and some severe. Animal guardians should always obtain professional examination, diagnosis and treatment by their veterinarian.

When an animal is more peaceful and calm through a Reiki session and beyond, then the natural internal healing processes can function better, complementary to veterinary care. Reiki does not cure the incurable, but

Rosina Maria Arquati: The Life Journey of an Animal Communicator

animals with serious illnesses can be less stressed and more relaxed so that they can be happier.

Reiki can also help to calm an animal when the guardian is giving medicines, relax when stressed, and soothe when under veterinary care.

How does it work?

Reiki is a form of laying on the hands. Reiki helps to balance "chakras" within the animal body. But, what are chakras and how do they exert their influence?

Chakras are energy centers located in a relatively straight line along the animal body. The word "chakra" means "wheel" and chakras are pictured as spinning wheels of energy. Chakras are believed to influence, both emotionally and physically, every part and function of the animal. Chakras are perceived as varying in brightness, depth and size depending upon health and vitality.

The concept of Chakras is as follows. Although the animal body contains a number of energy points, there are seven main Chakra centers in the animal aura. Through the seven chakras, animals receive and give off essential energy between the physical and subtle bodies. An animal's thoughts and feelings filter down through the chakras to the physical animal body, where they become outer manifestations.

A balance within the chakras results in optimal health and vitality. It is through the chakra network that the animal's mind, body, and spirit interact as one holistic system. Damage to one of the chakras through trauma, injury, emotional conflict, or other means, is believed to manifest as dysfunction in the related area of the physical animal body. The purpose of using Reiki is to restore the balance of subtle energies and help towards returning the physical animal being to a healthy state.

Reiki FAQ (靈氣常見問題)

1. Please describe Reiki to someone who has never heard about it?

   Reiki is a traditional Japanese art of healing. It channels the universe's life force energy to heal and strengthen. It is a spiritual technique that communicates with bodies, whether human or animal, at the deepest level. It is commonly called palm healing, where our hands act as funnels, transferring the universe's energy into the animal or person. The word "Reiki" is made of two Japanese words—Rei which means "universal" and Ki which is "vital life force energy". Therefore, Reiki is actually "Universal life force energy."

2. When do you use Reiki on animals? In what situation?

   Reiki, for the animals, can be used in many situations—stress, anxiety, pain, old age, sickness; in fact in almost any situation. There is no harm in receiving Reiki and it is beneficial to the animals. It can also be used on a regular basis, as maintenance, even on a well and healthy animal.

3. What do you do exactly to the animal?

   You place your hands on the animals to give them Reiki. It is not necessary to touch them as some animals might be too sick or stressed to be touched. It works equally well without having to lay your hands on the animals.

4. What do you think the animal feels?

   For humans, we sometimes feel heat or coolness from the hands of a Reiki practitioner and animals would feel that too. Sometimes tingling sensations may be experienced.

Rosina Maria Arquati: The Life Journey of an Animal Communicator

5. What is the reaction?

Most animals love and enjoy Reiki. Cats especially are known to love it. You can see their reactions almost instantly—they would either calm down, fall asleep or even turn their bodies to you for Reiki. The animals would know which part of their body requires Reiki most and would turn that part towards you for healing.

6. How effective is it?

With some animals, you can see them visibly feeling better in just a single session. With other animals, it might take a few regular sessions to help them to feel better and more comfortable.

7. What are the results?

The results are wonderful, or else I would not be practising Reiki on so many animals, and people would not be asking for such services or taking up courses to learn Reiki from me so that their pets can benefit more too.

8. Please provide an example.

I was part of a rescue mission for an injured street dog, Venus. According to people who witnessed the accident, she was apparently hit and dragged by a car. She was just about a year old. When I saw her at the veterinary hospital, she was in pain, highly stressed and visibly upset. I knelt beside her cage and gave her some Reiki. She then turned around in her cage and turned her rear towards me for Reiki. Just then, the doctor [veterinarian] came out and informed us that Venus, the street dog was actually pregnant and in the accident, she lost all her babies. She was hurting and she turned her rear to me for Reiki. It was truly a touching and amazing experience. Animals do know you mean well.

Reiki helps remind us of who we are beneath the stresses, worries and judgments of the modern world. It draws attention to the ways in which we are limiting ourselves and our experience of life. It has the ability to awaken our awareness. It can remind us of our potential. Reiki complements other therapies.

Reiki is awareness: awareness of body, awareness of mind, awareness of yourself, and your relationship with the world.

Often the origins of a physical disease are to be found within, in our thoughts, our habits, the ways in which we condition ourselves to act in daily life. Thus, by becoming aware, we allow the possibility of change. That is true healing.

There may be short term discomfort but, if so, it relates to the beneficial effects of Reiki. For example, temporary aches due to increased circulation in an arthritic joint where circulation has been poor for many years.

The Reiki experience is a personal one. It is different for each individual.

Reiki is not a religion. It has been used by practitioners of Christianity, Buddhism, Hinduism and Islam. It is a spiritual practice that complements any faith as a hands-on healing practice.

A sick pet needs the love, care, and support of his/her human companions. At the same time, when their pet is ill, people may become distressed and worried, building up negative energy which can affect both the people and the animal. This in turn can adversely affect the healing progress of the pet. In many cases, therefore, it is beneficial for a pet to be given Energy Healing together with his/her human companion(s).

Energy Healing is a complementary therapy, and so it can be used alongside conventional veterinary treatment. It is never a substitute for diagnosis and treatment by a registered veterinarian.

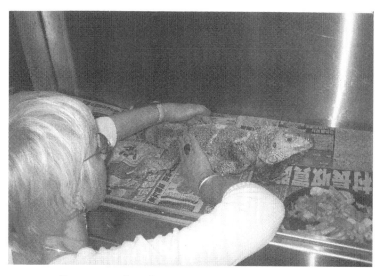

Energy Healing for Iguana in a veterinary clinic

Energy Healing for Dog

Energy Healing for a sphinx cat

Animal Welfare

Living in Peace and Harmony with Animals and Nature

To move towards the ideal of living in peace and harmony, we need to come to value and protect the lives and well-being of animals, the whole Animal Kingdom, and learn to live in ways which help and protect Nature without doing harm. The will to live is substantial in non-human animals as it is in our species *Homo sapiens* [humans].

Yet we humans as a whole, across Planet Earth, have taken it upon ourselves to decide the fates, life or death, of millions of innocent animals every year, killing so-called "surplus/unwanted animals", slaughtering animals for our stomachs, hunting, shooting, trapping, fishing, and more. Millions of animals suffer/die at the hands of humans: in puppy farms, pet trade, bad zoos, farms, slaughterhouses, laboratories, and still more. Forests and other habitats are destroyed every year by humans. We pollute and damage Nature, and largely ignore the warnings from scientists that it is our life support system which we are harming.

Is this how we want to be? What we want to be?

"If we *(humans)* behave better, we have the power to make things better for everything else . . . . At the moment we are making things worse." [Attributed to Sir David Attenborough in a recent TV programme.]

Animal welfare, living in harmony, protecting Nature: these matters would take another book by itself to cover them all. I try to adopt a holistic and practical approach. This chapter briefly touches on some of the basics.

In Animal Communication we move towards developing a better empathy with animals, to better understand the animals. In this we must consider the welfare of the animals, and it is appropriate in this book about Animal Communication to include this brief chapter on animal welfare.

A Pet is for Life

When taking on an animal you need to be aware that "A pet is for life". It is a living sentient being, with feelings and emotions, sad, happy, just like us. A new puppy or kitten or other animal is not a plaything or fad to be abandoned when one tires of him/her. You are responsible for that life, that living being, for the rest of his/her life. A dog or cat can live 15-20 years. We now know that well cared for rabbits may live up to 10 years or so. A tortoise can live for many decades, some for more than a hundred years. Some parrots can live for several decades.

Beforehand, it is necessary to carefully consider many matters. Can you commit to this care for the whole life of the animal? Do your working hours now and in future allow you to provide sufficient care and to spend time with the animal? Will you be able to buy the proper food and other things? Are you able to pay veterinary bills for all those years? Is your home environment and situation suitable for the animal? Do local laws and rules allow you to keep the animal? Do you fully know and understand how to properly care for this animal? Does every member in the family want the animal? It is important that every family member does want the animal and is willing to put in the effort and commitment for life.

The Pet Trade

In recent decades, in many countries, puppy mills/farms, kitten mills/farms, etc, have mushroomed. Many of these keep the animals in poor conditions, often unhealthy, with in-breeding causing inherited diseases, and a lack of proper health and hygiene measures causing infectious diseases to spread.

In another sad side of the pet trade, trading in wild creatures, animals are caught in the wild, to be sold on as "pets". Many animals suffer and die in this process.

Feral Animals: Humane Animal Population Management.

(Reproduced with permission of Dr David Burrows, Hong Kong)

"Feral animals" is a term now widely used to describe populations of animals living as wild animals, but which originated from domestic animals which were lost or abandoned and managed to survive and produce self-sustaining wild-like populations of animals, generation upon generation. They are the result of past [and sometimes present] human malpractices.

For decades, humans have adopted the approach that they don't want the animals there, so the animals are caught and many are eventually killed, or simply killed in situ. This is the wrong approach. It causes much animal suffering, and unnecessary killing. It is almost impossible to remove every feral animal in this way, and the remaining animals simply reproduce faster with better survival of the offspring from reduced competition for food and resources.

Authorities in many countries attempt to justify this catch/remove/kill as necessary to prevent rabies. This is wrong. The *WHO Expert Consultation on Rabies, 5-8 October 2004*, held that dog destruction alone is not effective in rabies control and that there is no evidence that removal of dogs alone has ever had a significant impact on dog population densities or the spread of rabies. It further held that mass canine vaccination campaigns have been the most effective measure for controlling canine rabies. [WHO is the World Health Organization]

So, a paradigm shift is needed: "In order to reduce or stabilize the population of feral animals in a locality, we will put the animals back there." This is difficult for many people to understand. Mind set: "There are too many animals there, so get rid of them!"

But there is a guarantee! A properly spayed animal will never again produce offspring. An unspayed female cat and her mate and all their offspring, producing two litters per year with 2.8 surviving kittens per litter: in one year can produce more than ten extra cats, and in 5 years can produce many thousands of extra cats. (USA figure quoted from SPCA website in Hong Kong). In contrast, one properly spayed female cat and one properly neutered male cat will still total only two cats one year later, five years later, and so on. Similar calculations can be made for many species.

The Workforce. In many parts of the world, there is a huge army out there consisting of people who care about animals, who will enthusiastically do their share to save the animals through a well organized programme of humane population management. They need guidance and support, and it can work.

Guidelines setting out the Fundamentals can help to achieve consistent results and agreed programmes to success. Such guidelines were drawn up in Hong Kong more than a decade ago to keep a then embryonic programme on the right track. They are outlined here:-

1. Manage the animal population realistically Assess and define the existing population of animals Identify existing groups/colonies/distribution. Estimate the numbers, kinds and distribution/locations of the animals as accurately as possible. Identify locations

for feeding, trapping, shelter, etc, where they will not cause nuisance or problems. Prepare a practical programme plan which is achievable and realistic

2. Work to achieve a high percentage of sterilized animals in the population in a "short" time frame A low percentage of sterilized animals in a population is ineffective in controlling the numbers in a population group. Studies on TNR (trap/neuter/return) have given estimates of a need to sterilize between 70 % and 94 % of a population of cats or dogs. Animal colony carers may tend to be over-optimistic about their percentage achievements, so aim for 100%.

3. Manage the animals to avoid negative impact on wildlife and the environment. Conservationists are sometimes the biggest opponents of TNR programmes for ferals. TNR is for saving lives: not only cats and dogs but also to protect wild birds and other creatures. Feeding the TNR colony animals is part of this, so that the animals are not hungry and do not depend on hunting for food. Monitor the wildlife and environment, and work to achieve harmony insofar as is possible.

4. Local community support. The human community can sway politicians and officials. Communication to obtain on-going support is important for lasting success. Protect the human community: eg anti-rabies vaccination and health programmes for the animals.

5. Deal with nuisances or fear caused by animals in the programme. Nuisance or fear may be real or perceived, but are "real" to the complainants.

6. Good monitoring and care for the colony animals. Good carers. Food, water, care, monitoring. Always adopt a humane approach. Include health programmes and disease-prevention for the animals in the programme, identification, vaccination, etc.

7. Severely aggressive individual animals must be addressed. Usually there are very few such individuals, often none. But consider community fears and "hysteria", so a clear policy on such animals is needed.

8. Holistic approach. It is necessary to include measures to humanely manage matters such as colony immigration, new abandonments, neighbouring groups of animals, owned and loosely owned animals interacting. It is not just TNR, but also area ABC + RPO + health; and includes animal health, human health, safety, rabies prevention, and so on. [RPO is Responsible Pet Ownership. ABC is Animal Birth Control. TNR is Trap Neuter Return.]
9. Monitor progress, and implement humane corrective action when needed.
10. Keep good records of the programme. Write it up, scientifically if possible. Despite the many successful documented programmes of TNR/ABC etc, there is a dearth of write ups of these successful scientific studies in scientific journals.

[These paragraphs on feral animals were presented at Animals for Asia Conference, Chengdu 2011, and 1st International Conference on Dog Population Management, York 2012; presentations by Dr David Burrows, Veterinarian. Copyright Dr David Burrows Hong Kong, reproduced here with permission.]

Well-managed ABC/ TNR programmes can be adapted for many species. For example, wild monkey populations in Hong Kong which came into conflict with urban humans were (and are) addressed using in-situ contraceptive methods instead of spay/neuter.

Wildlife and Nature

For animals out in the wild, we must have sustainable environments for them to live. Areas with people must be balanced ecologically to live in harmony. We live in an ecosystem. Disappearance of species and habitats causes imbalances, so we should try to live harmoniously with all species and with nature.

To care for our brothers and sisters in the animal kingdom, we must care about our beautiful planet Mother Earth for the future health of ourselves and our children and grandchildren. We must look at the welfare of animals, of the planet, and of ourselves, to have a balanced world where we can all live balanced happy lives in harmony.

Human Overpopulation

As the human population continues to grow, our species further exhausts the resources of the planet, damages the environment, causes habitat destruction, animal suffering, and human suffering.

"*Homo sapiens* (us) is the only species which considers itself to have the right to control the populations of all other species whilst being completely unable to control our own population." [Attributed to Dr Bernard Grzimek, twentieth century zoologist in Germany.]

Testing.

Using animals for testing of products is cruel and inefficient. With new technology, tests can be developed using alternative methods. The development of humane alternatives is currently kept slow by a lack of funds, while large amounts of money continue to be pumped into animal testing.

Meat, Fish

The increase in intensive farming of animals is a cruel and ineffective way to feed the world. The use of antimicrobials and other drugs in intensive farming harms our health, and meat production is an inefficient way to produce protein. It is also harming our life-support system: the FAO has calculated that farming for meat produces around 18% of global warming gases. [FAO is the Food and Agriculture Organization of the United Nations].

Equally, the intensive fishing of seas is harming the seas and life in them, the birthplace of life on earth.

Fur

In this 21st century, with our many clothing options and choices, it seems archaic and barbaric to wear furs. Sharp-eyed readers will have noticed in the wedding photo on page 25 that my mother wore fur trim and my mother-in-law wore a fur coat.

This was embarrassing! Neither of them would do that nowadays.

Furs come from living sentient beings which are needlessly killed for their fur. Often the animals are kept in dreadful conditions. In recent years, undercover videos have revealed that sometimes the animals are skinned alive, which is hideous and unconscionable cruelty.

Do No Harm

A good Animal Communicator is a person who empathizes with animals. This empathy helps the Communicator to understand them. Empathy should properly lead to understanding and to sympathy, and sympathy relates to compassion. The compassionate person is opposed to cruelty. The compassionate person also wants to end suffering.

Meat production probably causes more animals to suffer than any other causes of suffering and cruelty. This is because so many millions of animals are used to produce meat every year.

In theory, people hope that the animals are raised and cared for humanely, then transported and killed nicely. For more than 99% of animals used to produce meat, it does not happen like this. Quite the opposite: cruelty and suffering are endemic in the processes of using animals as food. Eating meat continues the demand to use animals as food, and finances the systems which cause the cruelty and suffering.

Some people prefer to be ***speciesists***, treating dogs and cats and some other pet species differently from cattle, pigs, chickens, turkeys, fish and so on. The speciesist approach, sadly, continues the demand which finances the systems which cause the cruelty.

When the Animal Communicator communicates with an animal, the Communicator tries to become a friend of the animal. Do we eat our friends? Instead, it is better to *Live and Let Live*.

Becoming vegan helps the Animal Communicator to play a part in reducing cruelty and suffering, and to consciously and subconsciously feel goodness and compassion towards all animals, to empathize with animals, and to transmit feelings of kindness and understanding to the animals.

Keep On, Don't Give Up

Putting this book together seems to be an endless project, so it has been decided to end here with another book to follow.

I hope that you have enjoyed reading my life story and following my introduction into animal communication.

In this book I have set out the basics of animal communication. However, many people find it difficult to learn this from a book, and progress better in classes and workshops interacting with classmates of like mind, and with the teacher. To continue the journey you may wish to join classes and workshops.

Always remember that animal communication is for good, for kindness, for compassion. It should never be abused to exploit or harm people, animals or nature.

I hope that you are inspired to take up the challenge of talking to animals. Remember, this is a fun and wonderful experience which can change your life for the better.

I look forward to seeing you at workshops and classes, or in contact via the internet, and sharing your wonderful experiences.

And may your life be filled, as mine has, through wonderful communications with our brothers and sisters in the Animal Kingdom.

Namaste
Rosina

Rats have feelings too. Pet rat in a veterinary clinic

PART III
Appendix

Animal Communication Practice Log Sheet Proforma

Use the log sheet proforma on the next page to record your animal communication experiences.

This will help you to understand the ways in which you communicate with animals, and how different animals communicate with you.

Basic Animal Communication Log Sheet Proforma

Note down your animal communication experiences, and tick or comment for each category experienced.

Date   **Animal**   **Question**   **Answer**   Interpretation

Category: Picture[s] Words Sentence Feelings Smell Video Other

---

Date   **Animal**   **Question**   **Answer**   Interpretation

Category: Picture[s] Words Sentence Feelings Smell Video Other

---

Date   **Animal**   **Question**   **Answer**   Interpretation

Category: Picture[s] Words Sentence Feelings Smell Video Other

---

Date   **Animal**   **Question**   **Answer**   Interpretation

Category: Picture[s] Words Sentence Feelings Smell Video Other

---

ACKNOWLEDGEMENTS

I wish to thank all those people in the early days who helped me to bring Animal Communication to the forefront in Hong Kong.

Animal Communication continued to grow, and I thank those who stayed with me or joined me to move Animal Communication ahead to where it is today. Many are still with me, and they have my thanks.

I thank my Hong Kong coordinator who has worked with me through many difficult times, and who readily answers telephone and email communications when animals are lost, sick, or otherwise need help.

I also thank the people in Singapore, Taiwan, Malaysia and elsewhere who helped me to bring Animal Communication to the forefront in their countries, and those who continue to do so.

My thanks go to the coordinators in Singapore, Taiwan and Malaysia who coordinate our animal communication workshops and the efforts there to help animals.

My thanks also go to the coordinator of AACCA whom I so value in fundraising work for charities, and those who work with her at the charity events to raise funds to help animals. [AACCA is the Alliance of Animal Communicators Caring about Animals.]

I thank all the students of Animal Communication who have opened their hearts to the Animal Kingdom and to communicating with animals.

Thanks also go to the translators, to those who write heartwarming and compassionate articles for our newsletters, and to others who help.

My thanks also go to the lost animal teams, who give their time to help to reunite animals with their humans.

I further thank my publishers.

Thanks go to my veterinarian husband, who is also my spellcheck and veterinary advisor.

I thank my wonderful animal guides White Ray of Beauty and Tenderfoot, and my native american guide Rainbow Warrior.

I send my thanks to all those animals over so many years who have spent time communicating with me or with my students.

I thank them all from the bottom of my heart as without them I could not do the work I do now.

Namaste,
Rosina

Rosina Maria Arquati

Animal Talk Ltd

Animal Communicator and Animal Healer
Animal Communication Workshops/Classes
Bereavement Counselor

Phone (mobile)	(+852) 6089 4727 (English, Cantonese, Mandarin/ Putonghua)
Landline	(+852) 2549 3332 (English)

Email	animaltalk8@gmail.com
Website	http://rosina.wordpress.com
China web	http://blog.sina.com.cn/animaltalk

Come and Join Rosina Arquati Facebook (Official):

http://www.facebook.com/rosina.arquati
http://www.facebook.com/#!/pages/Animal-Talk-Asia/15536
1161293637

Main email address   (international)

animaltalk8@gmail.com

Local email addresses

Hong Kong:	animaltalk8@gmail.com
Taiwan:	animaltalktw@gmail.com
Malaysia:	animaltalkmalay@gmail.com
Singapore:	animaltalksg@gmail.com
China:	animaltalkchina@gmail.com

Printed in Great Britain
by Amazon